# Kinds of Prayer:
# Knowing Them and Using
# Them Effectively

## Chris A. Legebow
## Living Word

This book explains the kinds of prayer to get the most effective results.

ISBN: CANADA  978-0-9952715-1-7

# DEDICATION

I thank God for the teachers and preachers who broadcast the gospel faithfully from their pulpits or their TV studios, throughout North America and the rest of the globe. I especially  thank the Apostles, Prophets, Pastors, Teachers and Evangelists who flow in their gifts imparting an anointed Word. I thank you servants, encouragers, givers, mercies, leaders. I thank God for Christian Media and  Entertainment. I thank God for the local churches I have been part of.   All of these members of The Body of Christ have contributed to my spiritual life.

# CONTENTS

# ACKNOWLEDGMENTS

All Scripture taken from Biblegateway.com
King James Version (KJV)
Modern English Version (MEV)
New International Version (NIV)

# 1 INTRODUCTION TO KINDS OF PRAYER

My prayer in writing this book is that I could pass on to others those Spiritual truths that I have been taught by faithful servants of God, so they also could pass them on to others. This book is meant for Christians; specifically, it is meant for born again – spirit filled Christians who want to know more about God and more about prayer. About 20 years ago I was introduced to a book that revolutionized my prayer life. I will refer to that book here as an excellent resource; It is Effective Fervent Prayer by Mary Alice Isleib. The book describes different types of prayers. She compares the different methods of prayer to different types of equipment used for different sports. It is an excellent analogy.

James 5; 16 Confess your faults to one another and pray for one another, that you may be healed. The effective, fervent prayer of a righteous man accomplishes much.

I was a person who was praying. I did get some results. I had read various books on prayer before that book but I didn't actually know there were different types used for different situations. People who want to know how to pray effectively should read that book. I am writing a book on kinds of prayer similar yet different as I describe in detail the various types of prayer I have experienced results with before and after I read that book.

Knowing that your prayer is heard is important. You may think God and answers all prayer. A person not praying in faith, or complaining to God will not achieve effective results. Effective prayer is prayer that God hears and answers. The scripture says that if we know He has heard us, we can know that we have the petitions we have asked of Him.

1 John 5: 14 This is the confidence that we have in Him, that if we ask anything according to His will, He hears us. 15 So if we know that He hears whatever we ask, we know that we have whatever we asked of Him.

What is Effective Prayer?

Effective means that it has accomplished what it was sent to do. It means answers have been released. God's word instructs us to pray in various ways for different situations. Fervency means passionate consistent prayer. Sometimes it means to pray and pray and pray until the answer manifests. Sometimes, with the prayer of faith, it means praying once and thanking God for the answer.

Luke 11: 9 "And I tell you, ask, and it will be given to you; seek, and you will find; knock, and it will be opened to you. 10 For everyone who asks receives, and he who seeks finds, and to him who knocks it will be opened.

Some prayer answers come immediately after we pray. Fervent means we don't give up – we pray believing God hears and answers prayer. An example of consistent passionate prayer is the Church in the book of Acts. The Church was praying for Peter's release from prison. They knew Peter had been taken and thrown into prison. They began praying for a miracle; they did not stop praying until he appeared at their door. God sent an angel who broke the chains off Peter and lead him out safely; the Church was surprised at his appearance. Because it was a miraculous answer to prayer.

Acts 12: 12: 16 But Peter continued knocking. And when they opened the door and saw him, they were astonished.

They were surprised because they did not know that God would answer the prayer so quickly, so miraculously and so excellently. Prayer can transform things: the supernatural can supersede all the laws of the natural realm. If there is no answer, God can create a way where there was no way.

Faith is a Factor

Effective prayer must be with faith. You must believe that God is and that He is a rewarder of those who seek Him. (Hebrews 11: 6). Without faith, it is impossible to please God. I emphasize it is impossible to please God without faith. How important is faith with prayer!

It is not a matter of repetitious prayer. In some denominations, certain prayers are done some many times as though the repetition would please God. Jesus tells us the following:

Matthew 6: 7 But when you pray, do not use vain repetitions, as the heathen do. For they think that they will be heard for their much speaking. 8 Do not be like them, for your Father knows what things you have need of before you ask Him.

Some denominations have books of prayer, in case people don't know what to pray. People turn to the prayer and read it to God. I am not completely against this. Faith must be attached to the prayer or it is simply a nice poem read to God. Other religions spin prayer wheels believing it will certainly get an answer from God. Quantity does not bring about an answer to prayer. The quality or sincerity of the faith of the prayer moves God. Faith moves God.

It says God knows the things we need before we pray. You may wonder if He knows what we need why are we praying. God instructs us to ask Him, even that He knows what we need. It is a sign of our faith in Him not only to Him but to the angelic realm that we cannot see with our physical eye.

The Joy of Prayer

Once you pray and realize God answers prayer, you will want to pray more. Please don't believe the lie that prayer is like some kind of duty or ritual. Prayer is exciting because as we pray, God shows up and His presence is so strong that we are overwhelmed with joy and peace and love. There is much pleasure in God's presence.

Psalm 16: 11 You will make known to me the path of life;
in Your presence is fullness of joy;
at Your right hand there are pleasures for evermore.

Petition

You may start your prayer life asking God for things; these are your petitions: for people's health, for others needs for your own self, but once you realize Almighty God of heaven and earth shows up in your prayers and literally helps you to pray, you will want to pray because of God. You will want to share His heart and start praying about things He cares about. You will start loving what He loves. You will grow in the depth of your relationship with God. You will be transformed from glory to glory. Prayer is speaking to God and Him speaking to you. It is a communication with God – that is not one way. God speaks to us also. Prayer is two – way communication. Hearing from God is the key. God could speak a word to you that will immediately transform you or give you direction. He delights in communing with His people.

John 10: 14 "I am the good shepherd. I know My sheep and am known by My own.

The Disciples' Prayer

The people who followed Jesus knew that He knew how to pray. They knew because they saw the healings and the miracles. They knew because he was constantly talking about God. They saw the evidence of His prayer life in his life and in those He had opportunity to share with. They begged Him to teach them to pray. Most of us know this prayer even if we only know one prayer. Usually, it is called the LORD`s prayer but in reality it is the disciples' prayer. Those who believe in the Lord can pray it.

Matthew 6: 9 "Therefore pray in this manner:
Our Father who is in heaven,
hallowed be Your name.
10 Your kingdom come;
Your will be done``
on earth, as it is in heaven.
11 Give us this day our daily bread.
12 And forgive us our debts,
as we forgive our debtors.
13 And lead us not into temptation,
but deliver us from evil.
For Yours is the kingdom and the power and the glory forever. Amen.`

This is an excellent prayer. It covers most aspects of our human lives. Pastor Larry Lea taught on this several decades ago and has an excellent book on prayer called `Could you not tarry One Hour`` Each chapter of the book covers a different part of the LORD`s prayer. I highly recommend that book to you.

This teaching is no way in the same depth or emphasis, but there are several areas of the LORD`s prayer. First it is acknowledging God as our Creator and ruler:
Vs 9 Our Father who is in heaven,
hallowed be Your name.

Truly let those words fill you. He is the creator of all yet He cares for each one of us personally.

Vs 10 10 Your kingdom come;
Your will be done``

on earth, as it is in heaven.

This causes us to know that God has a plan for our lives and for the earth. His will is that all people would come to the saving knowledge of Christ – but He will never violate a human will. He will not force anyone to believe. We can pray that He reveal Himself to people, that their hearts will be softened to want to know more of God. We can pray for God`s promise that Jesus is coming back again to set up His throne in Jerusalem and He will reign on the earth.

Vs 11 11 Give us this day our daily bread.

We should ask God to meet our daily needs. This includes literal bread – food but also needs such as a home, a job, a car etc. This is an aspect of the prayer of petition. We who are His children can ask God to supply our needs. God knows we need them but as an act of our faith in Him and His ability to supply, we ask Him for those needs. Also, thank Him for supplying. Never forget that God is the God who supplies all things that you have in life. He is the source of supply.

Philippians 4: 19 But my God shall supply your every need according to His riches in glory by Christ Jesus.

Vs 12 12 And forgive us our debts,
as we forgive our debtors

God has given us free will. He will never force you to do anything. Did you know that unforgiveness will block your prayer life? If you do not forgive, you cannot be forgiven. Some people have lived through horrendous things no person on earth should ever have to live through should he or she have a loving Christian family. The depths of the love of God can heal any person of anything he or she has ever experienced. God`s love is so miraculously healing and transformational that any residue or garbage attached to someone`s past can be completely wiped away as though it never happened.

If you haven`t heard of Joyce Meyer`s testimony of her childhood and how God completely healed and delivered her and transformed her so that she could totally forgive sexual abuse, you should get her books and watch her DVD;s. I have known people who have received deep inner healing of things done to them in their past because of her teachings. Because she is a living witness of God`s miraculous healing and deliverance and anointing and resurrection – she can speak so that others can be set free.

You may say but you do not know what was done to me. Jesus is our example. From the cross, He prayed that we who crucified Him might be forgiven. In His dying moments, He prayed forgiveness for us. He commands us to forgive. You may have to say it in faith (meaning you don`t feel it yet) but say it. Start praying for that person or people who did wrong to you and you will begin to feel love towards them. Your spirit must make your human will obey. You do it by faith until it is no longer a sore spot. You will know you are healed when you harbor no bitterness or resentment towards them. Please know I am not telling you to stay in an abusive situation. Don`t stay in such a place. Forgiveness doesn`t mean you go back to those who used or abused you but it does mean that you are free of their effects on your life.

Vs 13 And lead us not into temptation,
but deliver us from evil.

Praying to be on the right path, going the right way is essential. What I mean is there will always be temptations possible. We do not have to live in bondage to them. Things that once tempted you before do not need to keep a hold on you. God wants you to be free from any addiction or bondage. There is such a thing as total deliverance. This means whatever addiction you had no longer has a hold on you.

If you were not born in a Christian family, you may be tempted in areas others are not. Pray for God to deliver you from it. Get into a strong Christian Church that believes in healing and deliverance. Get some preaching and teaching on living a Holy life. Invest scripture into your life.

Vs 13 continued
' For Yours is the kingdom and the power and the glory forever. Amen.`

I kept this part separate because it is a full confession that God rules over all. It gives God glory. We should in our prayers always thank God for hearing and answering prayer. Thanking God for the answer is a special way of showing faith. It releases joy in your spirit to thank God. It releases faith in your heart to thank Him before the miracle manifests.

This prayer is an excellent way to show our love and trust for God; Jesus gave it as an example to us. We should pray it but It is not the only type of prayer, There are different types of prayer. Just as I have different types of sporting equipment for different sports I play, there are different types of prayers for different reasons.

This book is to teach some of the different types of prayer to help people pray effectively: to get results – answers to prayer. Prayer will increase your intimacy with God. You will come to know Him in a different light with each type of prayer you pray. Praying is communion with God – oneness. You will come to learn more about Him as you pray: you will be transformed in your spirit from glory to glory.
God Cares What You Care About

God cares about the things you care about. Don`t ever believe the lie that it`s too big for God to handle or too small for God to care about.

John 14: 13 I will do whatever you ask in My name, that the Father may be glorified in the Son. 14 If you ask anything in My name, I will do it.

Once in my first year of becoming a first-generation Christian, I was walking by myself and the flash of a thought came to me that I would like a cup of coffee at that coffee shop. I remembered I didn`t have enough money for a coffee. I was thinking to myself in my own self. I felt a shutter of self-pity. Almost immediately, less than a couple of minutes later, I saw a friend from school. She greeted me so warmly I forgot my self-pity. You may not believe this but she said ``Come on I`ll buy you a coffee.`` She did. I immediately realized God cared about something that may completely seem insignificant to anyone except me. I learned that no matter how small it might seem, I should pray. Also, there have been instances of praying literally in a life or death situation for someone, I believed God and His word rather than any negative report that I heard. I have seen God heal people who were at the brink of death or who were not given a chance of recovery, but God heard our prayers and healed them. I will discuss some of these situations in more detail in other parts of the book, specifically the prayer of faith.

Scripture as the Authority

What are you asking from God? Does it come in line with scripture? God`s Word, the Holy Bible, is the highest authority for God`s will on the earth, He will never go against His Word. If you are asking for something from God that is wrong or sinful or that violates someone else`s human will, God will not give it to you. God wants what is best for us. If we choose something that will kill us God will not give it to us.

Romans 6: 23 For the wages of sin is death, but the gift of God is eternal life through Jesus Christ our Lord.

Be Specific for What you Pray for.

God wants us to prosper; He will not go against His Word to us. If you ask something general from God, you might receive a general response such as `God bless me`. If you go to a fast food restaurant and order a hamburger. Most likely the clerk will ask you which one? What do you want on it? Would you like a drink with it? Do you want French fries? All those specific questions will arise because of one general request. If you specifically say you want Combo no. 4 with fries and a cola. You will get more specific service. God wants us to be specific with what we are asking from Him.

If you want a new car – search through webpages or magazines and see the type of car you want. Pray with faith believing God will honour your request. This is a prayer of petition. It is similar to asking to supply our needs. Jerry Savelle has an excellent book on prayer called The Prayer of Petition. Some many people are ignorant of this type of prayer. They may think that God would get them a cheap car but not an expensive car. They may think it is not right to ask for God what you want. If it comes into agreement with God`s Word (doesn`t sin or violate someone else) God wants to give it to you.

The answer will manifest if you, pray in faith believing. Find a Scripture to pray concerning the petition. You should write it in your prayer journal. Write the date. Get a picture of the thing you are believing God for and pray. You could sow a gift of faith praying over the finances to be a blessing to some deserving ministry. What you`ve done is you attached a gift offering of faith towards that thing you desire. It is usually money but it could be any act of giving to God.

Sow a Seed of Faith

The prayer of petition is a prayer that releases faith often with a financial gift; it speaks God`s language of faith. It shows God you are serious about it. Before I knew the proper term for this type of prayer, God revealed it to me. That is how I got my first computer. I saw it in a magazine. I wanted it. It would only be good for me and was completely in alignment with God`s word because it wasn't sinful. I didn`t have money to buy that computer. My desire for it was ridiculous. I was in debt for all my education. I had student loans to pay back. I was barely scraping by. I kept a picture of that computer and would look at it, and in my heart I believed I would get it. I didn`t know about praying the prayer of petition but I knew God cared enough for what I wanted that He cared if I had a cup of coffee or not.

Within one year of that first petition, I purchased the very computer that I did not know where the money would come from to pay for it. I also got a printer. Now to us today that seems like such a minor request. It wasn`t to me. Because I was a teacher, I had to stay at school late into the evening so I could use the school`s computer. Once I got my own computer, I could do my school work at home. It made all the difference to me. I thanked God for it. Thanking God after receiving a petition is as important as praying or as important as sowing a seed of faith.

Align With God`s Word

When I talk of asking specifically from God, some people get doubtful. For instance, a person may say `What if it is not God`s will for me to prosper? That would show the person has not read the scriptures. The book of Deuteronomy talks about God`s desire to bless His people. It is a religious lie that God want you poor. You must change your thinking so that you know God wants the best for you. God wants you to have the best – more awesome than what you can imagine for your own self.

Luke 12: 32 "Do not be afraid, little flock, for it is your Father's good pleasure to give you the kingdom

God`s Word Must Become Important

God`s Word is our basis for our prayer life. Reading God`s Word helps us to know His will. If we pray outside the Word of God, God will not give us our request. If you ask to control someone`s life or will, you are sinning. God will never force a person to accept Him; He draws people unto Himself and we must willfully desire Christ as Saviour. He most certainly will not violate someone`s human will to answer your prayer. You should know it is a sin and repent if you have done it. God will give you the best, but you cannot ask God to violate His Word. His Word expresses His will.

You can pray for God to soften the person`s heart towards you. You can pray that you have an opportunity to have a chance to speak with a person, but you should never pray – God change that person so he or she will do what I want. You cannot pray for your will to be above someone else`s will. You must ask within the will of God – from Genesis to Revelation God expresses His will for all people on earth. He reveals Himself to us through the covenants He has made with different people. Jesus brought the New Covenant, making it possible for you and I to enter the Holy of Holies – we are not only His servants but we are His sons and daughters. We are His family. In fact, Jesus says we are His body on the earth.

Find a Translation of the Bible you Can Read

I like the King James Version of the Bible, but not all people understand it. There are so many versions of the Bible available. Quite popular is the NIV version. The message version is in modern day language. The Amplified Bible is excellent for serious Bible study. I am using The MEV version in this book. I like it because it preserves the meaning of the King James but uses modern English. If you cannot understand the version of the Bible you are reading, it is no good for you. Get yourself a translation you can understand.

So, whatsoever we ask in the prayer of petition, we shall receive…. Ohhh as long as it is in God`s will; it must line up and not violate scripture.

God says Ask, Seek and Knock. Are you asking of God?

Matthew 7: 7 "Ask and it will be given to you; seek and you will find; knock and it will be opened to you. 8 For everyone who asks receives, and he who seeks finds, and to him who knocks, it will be opened.

Prayer and Praise

What are you asking? If you have nothing to ask, then you should be thanking Him. That means He has supplied all your needs. You should be praising and thanking God for what He has given you. Thanksgiving is a way of releasing joy within your own spirit because as you realize God has supplied for you, you realize the tremendous things He has done for you.

Seeking God

You may start seeking God for a petition to be granted but after He supplies it, you should seek Him to thank Him and to learn from Him. Seeking Him means you choose to draw close to Him. His presence alone is reason to seek Him. Certainly, Intercessory prayer or praying for others is important; I will talk more about it later in the book. Seeking God just to be in His presence praising and worshipping Him is a realm of prayer on its own. Miracles can occur because of the glory that manifest as God`s people are praising and worshipping Him. Gifts of the Spirit can manifest.

Make a Decision to Pray

To be practical, you must make a decision. Say within your spirit, I will seek the LORD each day. I will pray. Even if you start with a short space of time, you can develop your prayer life so it can involve more than one type of prayer. You can be praising and worshipping and making petitions and interceding and praying the prayer of faith etc, over hours that seem but as moments because of the glory of the LORD. Are you too busy for prayer? Your too busy. I like what Pastor Yonggi Cho of the largest church in Korea says. His Church has about 100, 000 members. He prays at least 3 hours a day. Reporters asked him what he does if his schedule gets really busy and he can`t fit the 3 hours into his day. If he can`t fit 3 hours of prayer in his schedule – he gets up early and prayer 6 hours instead knowing he needs extra from God to help him through the day.

His Church is famous for their devotion in prayer and winning souls. They have a mountain they go to and they fast and pray for days. If you have not read any of His books, I highly recommend them to you.

Prayer is not something we do recreationally – although there is much pleasure in prayer. It is something we do because we are communing with the LORD God almighty who can move heaven and earth to bring His will to come to pass. God can send angels to minister to people.

How to start a consistent prayer life

For new believers it may be 5 minutes or fifteen minutes. You should enter in with thanksgiving. You should praise God. If you have petitions, you should make them. You should thank God and praise Him at the end.

Psalm 100: 4 Enter into His gates with thanksgiving,
and into His courts with praise;
be thankful to Him, and bless His name.

Once you begin to receive answers from God, the compassion of God will well up inside of you and overflow so you will begin praying for people. You will care that others come to Christ. You will care that people`s needs

are met. You will want to pray for people because you know God answers prayer.

Consistently

As a new believer, first generation Christian, I would pray sometimes for hours and sometimes for less than five minutes. It depended on what I was doing and who I was with. At some point in those early years, I made a decision to set apart so much time each day. Usually, I start the day and end the day with prayer. I'm not saying you have to do it. First thing in the day is best for most people.

I heard Gloria Copeland say 'Consistency is the key to victory' It is so true. What we do each day shapes who we are. We decide to give ourselves to God each day. We decide to praise Him etc. This should mean we do not allow interruptions. We should turn off the phone, not answer the door or anything. For new Christians, you may find your mind tries to wander, Keep a pad of paper and a pen with you. If the thought comes to clean the garage, write it down. You can ask God to help you do those things on that list after you've prayed.

Seeking God means repeatedly. It is not once only. You seek God continuously. There is a story in the Bible of Elijah 1 Kings 18: 41b
And Elijah went up to the top of Carmel, and he threw himself down on the ground and put his face between his knees.
43 And he said to his servant, "Go up now, and look toward the sea."
And he went up and looked and said, "There is nothing."
And he said, "Go again," seven times.
44 On the seventh time, he said, "A small cloud as small as a man's hand is rising out of the sea."

They had drought for three years in that land because of the Word of the Lord through this prophet. God sent him to Ahab (the evil king) and prophesy that it was going to rain. The prophet went up on the mountain to pray and he started praying and praying; he sent his servant to see if there was any rain. The servant went once, twice and finally the seventh time; Elijah did not stop praying until He heard from his servant that a cloud about the size of a man's hand formed in the sky and was coming towards them. Do you know how small that speck of a cloud was?

The size of a man's hand isn't very big, but listen if it hasn't rained and there is even a slight hope – we should rejoice knowing God has answered out prayer. It builds with momentum as it approaches and there is an outpouring of rain on the dry land. He was a co-labourer with God in bringing the release of rain to that land. This is an example of continuous and believing prayer. He was seeking God for that answer to prayer until the answer occurred. I was taught this type of continual seeking for a prayer was called tarrying or waiting on the LORD. Usually, if God speaks prophetically about something to you it is because God wants you to pray for it.

Seeking until you find

Seeking God is sometimes repetitious – I do not mean use the exact same words. I mean you can sometimes seek God for an answer more than once. Sometimes there is a continual praying and interceding until a breakthrough comes. The words are not the same. The prayers are not the same. The need or the issue is the same until God moves heaven and earth to bring the answer. You can engage your spirit with God`s Spirit more than once about some things until they manifest on the earth. Prayer Assignments

This type of tarrying or coming to God and praying through something could be compared to an assignment that you must complete. I had prayer assignments on more than one occasion. Some of them are long and some are short. It is something you know must be made right so you continuously pray about it until there is a resolution. It is like a gear shift in the car. When you engage a gear, a new level is released until the car is driving at the proper speed. Your spirit engages with God`s Spirit and you are a co-labourer together with the Hold Spirit praying for this thing.

There are other prayers such as the prayer of faith. You pray it once in faith believing and bam! It manifests immediately. You may not see it with your eyes immediately but you will see it with your faith immediately. There will be a release in your spirit and you will know you have it. Start praising God and thanking Him for the answers to prayer.

Knock

Knock and it shall be opened to you. What is this knocking that I am talking about? There are doors or entrance in the spirit realm. As we are praying we knock on those doors until they are opened. I know it sounds funny to someone who doesn`t know what I am talking about but there are doors of opportunities, doors or utterance, doors to the future. Those doors can manifest things on the earth such as jobs, preaching opportunities, favour etc. I am saying that God literally cares so much about these things in our life that He will present us with doors to pray about so the manifestation will occur on the earth. God always gives us a choice. We do not have to choose that door, but if we will pray for it, if we will go through those doors, people are on the other side of those doors. It always involves people. It could be people getting saved, people being helped, people hearing about God. There can be tremendous blessing released if we obey.

For instance, if you are a person that doesn`t presently have a job, I can tell you it is God`s will for you to have a job. God created us to work. Money is the currency on earth. If we don`t work, we don't eat. (Phil 3: 10) You should put together a good resume and cover letter. You should apply for jobs. You should do everything you can do. You should also pray and keep praying until you get your job. God won`t bless us if we don`t do our part. If there is something we can do, we should do it. Even simple things like creating a resume are important. At a point when I could not find a job, I put my hands on my resume and prayed over it – that God would open an opportunity for me.

Doors in the Spirit Realm

It is possible there may be hindrances to those doors. Our prayers literally are a repetitive knocking on the door with faith that God will open the right doors for us. I heard Marilyn Hickey actually teach `Say out loud, I am knocking on this door and it shall be opened to me`. That teaching changed the way I pray about knocking on the doors. I knew they existed. I knew they had to be prayed about but I hadn`t been taught about how to properly pray about it until that teaching.

I literally prayed that prayer of knocking on the door of heaven that a job opportunity would be given to me. I sowed a seed of faith believing for that job opportunity. I thank God that He removed all hindrances and opened an opportunity for me. When you are praying the prayer of knocking, you must do it with fervency. You should do it so you will be free to pray – not distracted by things. I say this because you can usually pray driving or walking or bathing or working. This special type of prayer though demands your full attention.

Friendships

You might wonder what this has to do with prayer but it does certainly. If you are a new Christian such as I once was with only the Christians at Church in my life, you may have to get rid of some of the other friends. If those people do not encourage you to press into God, if they do not encourage you to grow spiritually, they cannot be close to you. The people you associate determines who will be influencing you. Don't let somebody full of unbelief and doubt, with a carnal life influence you. You should pray for Christian friends – people you can pray with, people who will encourage you in your spiritual growth – not someone who will hinder you.

If you do not have those Christians in your life right now, stay alone. Seek God instead. God will release the right people of like precious faith into your life at the right moment. Keep building yourself up in the Holy faith by memorizing scripture, saying it, praying it, singing it. Keep your spirit fixed on God. Christian friends are too precious to settle for less than the best. You can motivate yourself with Christian preaching and teaching. You can connect with the Internet to get excellent Christian teaching and preaching and praise and worship and movies and media. You can be joined to other Christians. Keep your heart right. Keep encouraging your own self.

There are people who seek the same thing. They desire to serve God with all their being. They live for His glory. They are radical Christians – meaning they are all in for Christ. There is no compromise in them. They are born-again spirit filled and living to win people for Christ. These are the types of Christian friends we should be with. Ask God for these types of friends.

If you are not in a local church, get yourself in a local church that believes in the Bible. Find a spirit filled church that believes in the gifts of the Holy Spirit.

Get in a Place that Reveres God's Word

Get in a church that believes that the Bible is God's divine will expressed to us in human terms so that we can understand the Holy scriptures. Get yourself with people that want to pray. Get yourself into a spirit- filled prayer meeting. Don't go to just any prayer meeting. If you go to a prayer meeting where they say " If it be your will to heal,…" Get out of that place. God says I am the God that heals you (Exodus 15:26). We in Canada and the United States are privileged to get much Christian preaching and teaching on tv, satellite, radio, cable, the Internet. Some prayer meetings stream their meetings live. You can get in on some spirit filled meetings if you can't find it in your locality. There are excellent resources, excellent sources for you to get information from. Christian Broadcasting brings us not only teaching a preaching but also Christian world news and Christian entertainment.

Knock until you receive the answer. Knock and ask God to open doors of opportunity – financial or other. The Apostle Paul had a prayer request that doors of utterance (Col 4: 3) would be open to him. He wanted to share Christ with as many people as possible; his prayer request was for more opportunities.

What are you asking for? Are you seeking God? Are you knocking that it may be opened unto you?

Giving your Life to Pray for Something

There are people who give their whole lives to pray for people to be saved or for a nation to come to Christ. They may win 2 or 3 souls to Christ but they are praying for the nation to come to God. God stores our prayers in bowls near the altar of God. Not one prayer in faith is gone without being recorded and when those bowls are filled, they are poured out on the altar before God (Revelation 8: 4) It is as though certain things must occur before the fullness of the situation is manifest and the answer comes to earth; the people who come afterwards reap all the rewards of those prayers. I'm saying if you give your whole life praying for a situation and you don't see the answer with your physical eyes, it doesn't mean the answer won't come. God's timings are different than ours.

Praying for Loved ones to be Saved

First of all, God is merciful. He gives people so many chances to repent before He allows judgement on them. God will never force a person to accept Him. You can pray for a loved one all your life. Don't think nothing is happening because that person doesn't feel tuggings at his or her heart drawing him or her to God. With each prayer, God gives them opportunities to accept Him. Believe that even if the person dies and you haven't witnessed his or her salvation that at the end of the person's life God gives them a fresh opportunity. You could be praying and God will release angels; God will release people who will witness to them.

It is like there is a crust that is hard like a shell that is in that person's heart that stops him or her from receiving Christ. Continual prayer gives an opportunity for that part of their heart to be softened. Please remember though, the person must will it. God cares so much about our free will, He will not ever force us to receive Him. Fresh opportunities come, but we must say yes to God. Each softening of the heart is a display of God's mercy towards those people.

It's God's will that His glory would cover the whole earth as the waters cover the sea. (Habakkuk 2: 14) are you praying this? You could pray it for your city, for your province or state for your country. You could pray it over the continents of the earth. A day will come when it most certainly will occur. Jesus' throne will be in Jerusalem. He will rule and reign on earth. Praying for people allows chances for those people to come to Christ.

God can Often a Hard Heart

I am a gardener. The first turning of soil is not easy. It requires much digging and removal of stones etc. But the second turning and all the ones to follow are easier because once the ground is ploughed, the hard, compact clay is broken and the earth can be worked as you add nutrients and compost, good soil is the result. It is the same in the spirit. Once a person has been softened for the Lord, he or she must meet with someone who would share the gospel. So after you pray God soften their hearts, pray God release labourers.

There are some family members who won't come to Christ even though they see results in your life. They are stubborn and won't listen to you because they know you and they know you are not perfect and they knew you before you were saved. God can send someone else into their lives who will share Christ at a place where that person will not only listen but accept Christ.
Jesus Blood

Jesus blood shed for us on Calvary gives us boldness to pray and ask for ourselves and for others. We are as kings as priests to our God (Rev. 1: 6) . That means we have authority in both the natural realm – concerning our place of employment, our social life, our church, our associations and in the spiritual realm as a spiritual people purchased by God and consecrated or set apart for His glory.

Don't be ashamed to ask God for what you need or even for what you desire. Please though, don't stop there. Pray for others. There is so much joy in praying for others' needs and seeing answers to prayer. It is awesome that Almighty God uses vessels like you and I to be co-labourers with Him in eternal matters. Our prayers matter to God. To see God pouring out His Spirit on others and blessing others that you have been praying for is a joy that I can't quite describe. It releases joy in your own heart knowing that you were doing what God wanted you to do and you (and others) made a difference on the earth in someone's life.

Abiding

John 15: 7 If you remain in Me, and My words remain in you, you will ask whatever you desire, and it shall be done for you.

O there is an abiding – that is dwelling in Christ and Christ dwelling in you so strongly and so rightly that you will be prompted by the Holy Spirit and immediately obey. You will desire something and God will give it to you. Abiding in Christ means to live in the spirit and be lead by the spirit. I knew a man of God many years ago who had a glow about him. He was one of the people I used to pray with. He was an elder in the church not in name only.

He delighted in giving, in serving the LORD, in praying. He always seemed to know when I had no money, he would buy my dinner. It was supernatural really. He talked about the intimacy of God that comes from abiding in the presence of the LORD – not just dropping in for a visit but consistent intimate abiding with Christ.

This special man, imparted this scripture to me: He said If we are not living in Christ, abiding in Christ, living in the presence of the LORD, in the new covenant of His blood, sharing Christ, living for God with all your being; he said if you are not abiding, you won't receive. If you are abiding in Christ, you will surely receive. Are you abiding in Christ? Is Christ you dwelling place or some place you go to if you have a need. Are you living your life 100% consecrated to God? Are all actions of your life in accordance with God's will and purpose? You may think O that sounds like a robot. No. It is true freedom. Abiding in Christ is living free to choose and choosing Christ consistently. It is a place of blessing and favour. God is a God of covenant. He keeps His covenant. Jesus blood is the promise of that new covenant.

More on Prayer

Is there something that makes you want to know more about prayer? Is there some loved one you are praying for? You can pray effectively, fervently. You can pray with faith believing with confidence knowing that you are a making a difference.

Prayer of Salvation

If you do not know the LORD Jesus Christ as your personal Saviour, the good news is you can. If you are interested in this book on prayer and you are not a Christian, the Holy Spirit is drawing you to God. It is so easy to receive Jesus – but it will change your life forever.

Pray believing that Jesus died and rose from the dead and that His blood cleanses you from all sin and unrighteousness. Repent – tell God you are sorry, you repent, that is you turn away from your sin and you turn towards God. You will no longer do the sinful things you did. You will no longer be a part of anything that is wrong. You purpose in your heart to live for Jesus Christ.

You will not be the same if you sincerely pray this prayer. Your desires will be to please God and to live a righteous life. You will desire spiritual life – spiritual nourishment in God`s Word. You will be born into a spiritual family – The Church. You will desire the company of other Christians.

You become part of the family of God. You will never be alone because «Christ dwells within you.

A sample Prayer you Could Pray (with faith) as follows:

Lord Jesus, I know that I am a sinner. I believe that you died on the cross and that you rose from the dead and ascended into Heaven and are coming back again. I believe your blood washes me and cleanses me. I thank you for forgiving my sins. I give my life to you Jesus – come fill me and direct my steps. Help me with decision making. I pray in your name Jesus thanking you for saving me. Amen.

Start reading the Bible. It is God`s Word for humans and how we should live our lives on the earth. Get into a good local Church that believes God`s Word and teaches it with faith. Thank God you are part of the family of God. You have been born again from above – you have been transformed. You are a Christian.

Prayer for Baptism of the Holy Spirit

If you are a Christian but you are not yet baptized in the Holy Spirit, there is good news, you can be. The baptism of the Holy Spirit is for all Christians. God promised that He would pour out His Spirit on the Church. Acts 2 describes the fulfillment of this promise. But it was not only for those people, it is for you if you believe.

Acts 2: 38 Peter said to them, "Repent and be baptized, every one of you, in the name of Jesus Christ for the forgiveness of sins, and you shall receive the gift of the Holy Spirit. 39 For the promise is to you, and to your children, and to all who are far away, as many as the Lord our God will call."

Start thanking God for saving you. Praise God. If you know some praise and worship choruses, start singing them with sincerity of worship. Ask God to baptize you in the Holy Spirit. You can receive it right there in your home, or in a car or anywhere. I recommend you do it in home or Church because it is an experience that will overwhelm you with the love of God for you. You may cry or weep. Words in a different language will come to you – speak them. God is literally praying in you and through you. This is a language to use for prayer. Get into a full gospel Church – where they believe in the Baptism of the Holy Spirit.

Romans 8: 26 Likewise, the Spirit helps us in our weaknesses, for we do not know what to pray for as we ought, but the Spirit Himself intercedes for us with groanings too deep for words. 27 He who searches the hearts knows what the mind of the Spirit is, because He intercedes for the saints according to the will of God.

# 2 PRAYING KNOWING THE NAMES OF GOD

LORD – I AM that I AM – Jehovah

Our God is a personal God not some unknown entity. God is as close or more close and intimate than a parent. He is the source of our life, our planet etc. He chooses to reveal Himself as a personal friend. God cares for us and calls us His people and His children.

Rapha – The LORD our Healer – If you know that He is Jehovah the Healer, you know certainly He is not going to make you ill. It would go against His very nature.

Tsidkenu Jeremiah 23: 6 – The LORD our righteousness. Please understand that God called Himself our righteousness even before He revealed Himself as Jesus our Saviour. Salvation was the plan for us all along. God was making covenant with people and revealing Himself as our righteousness thousands of years before Jesus died on the cross. We could never be righteous or pure or Holy without God. He is our righteousness.

Leviticus 20: 7-8 Jehovah Kaddish the one who sanctifies us or sets us apart. In the New Testament we are called the Church which is the Greek Word Ecclesia which means called out ones" out of the world and into the kingdom of God. We are separate because of our God. We are people called out of darkness into His light. 1 Corinthians 1: 30 tells us this.

Judges 6: 24 Jehovah Shalom - He is the God of our peace. I have always thought this simply means peace. In recent years I have heard teaching that the Hebrew word literally means wholeness or completeness – nothing missing, nothing broken, oneness, perfection. The Peace that God brings surpasses anything on earth.

If we live according to the media reports or people's news or live according to our feelings, we will live an up and down life. Our peace is in the LORD. He can calm us and give us peace in any situation. Our God lives in our hearts – I'm not talking about the physical organ. I am talking about the inner most chamber of your being – the core of you – the living soul. You are a spirit, you have a soul (mind, will and emotions) and you live in your physical body – the one God gave you. Our God lives in us. He brings us peace.

In the midst of any situation, you can have peace because He is the peace maker. He manifests His peace with His presence.

Jehovah Shamma – Omnipresent – He is always present. He is everywhere. He is with me here. He is with me no matter where I go. He is with believers in other parts of the earth – all over the earth – living in us – simultaneously omnipresent. Ezekiel 48: 35 and Hebrews 13: 5.

Jehovah Rapha – the Healer Exodus 15 and 26 and Psalm 103: 3 Bless the LORD who heals all my diseases. If you don't have the faith to know that God is your healer, pray the scripture for yourself. I will talk about it in a different chapter but as we pray God\s word, it releases faith in us and it brings us into alignment with God's Word. Remember His Word is His will.

Just as much as you believe He forgives all your sins, you should believe He is your healer. The blood of Jesus cleanses our sin, heals us and delivers us. Isaiah 53 reveals our Saviour and Healer.

Isaiah 53: 5
But he was wounded for our transgressions,
he was bruised for our iniquities;
the chastisement of our peace was upon him,
and by his stripes we are healed.

If you do not know He is your healer, literally pray the scripture for yourself or the person who needs healing. I mean literally say the words to God saying " LORD you said that by your stripes we are healed. I pray for healing for…" God's Word releases faith in the believer. The more you confess and pray the scriptures, the more your faith will grow.

I learned this years ago. I knew the Lord and had studied about God quite a bit, but no one had ever taught me to pray the scriptures. I believed I knew how to pray but it was only the starting point of my Christian life. I believed I knew God pretty well. But what happened was something horrible. Somebody I cared about very much was at the point of death. It was my pastor. We used to have a prayer chain in that church and they phoned to tell me that my pastor was deathly ill.

People may react differently but my reaction was horror and prayer. I had never had this type of need before someone literally in a life or death situation. By the next day, I had prayed everything I knew how to pray. I prayed in English and prayed in tongues (that is a Godly language that God Himself gives you to use). I knew it wasn't enough. What I did is I started searching through my concordance on every scripture that had to do with healing. I believe God quickened it to me. I knew I needed ammunition from God's Word. I started proclaiming those scriptures over my pastor. I started praying God's word Knowing that God is the same yesterday, today and forever. I would pray " God you healed the woman with the issue of blood, you can heal my pastor…" I personalized it totally and gave me a whole new realm of prayer – praying scriptures over my pastor.

I wish I could tell you it was a one-time event but it wasn't. It was an assignment from God because I knew I had to do it. I knew it wasn't God's will for him to die. He was in the prime of life, had a church, kids and grandchildren. He had much word in him to share and I knew in my spirit it was not his time to die. I knew that he was under attack for his life. The prayer assignment was a process of 2 years.

The doctors had given him a negative report saying he would not live or if he did live he could be a vegetable. They said he might not be able to walk or preach again. I want to say I am one of the people God gave the assignment to. There were a core of us who gathered every day until he was completely healed. At first the church was so crowded there was barely room to get a seat. Other Pastors of other churches came to pray for him. People loved him. But there were a core of us who continued and continued, not accepting any negative report but believing in God's Word for complete healing for him.

This engaging in prayer and praying through a situation was once called "praying through" a situation. The Latter rain movement is my history as I come from a Church birthed before it and famous for it. During WW II, people would go to the church every day praying for the safety of their loved ones and of our troops.

Prayer Assignments

Praying through is something that happens when the prayer is not easily answered in one day or two days. You know that it is the will of the LORD for the people to live or be safe etc. Your spirit engages with God's Spirit and you come into agreement with God concerning the situation UNTIL the situation changes, It is a prayer assignment. Not everyone accepts it. You don't have to accept it. God never forces you. But if God is calling you to pray for something like this, it can mean tremendous blessing for the person or people you are praying for but also yourself. God will richly bless you with more than you can imagine spiritually. You learn about things you would never know had you not accepted the prayer assignment.

As sure as I know an assignment from my workplace has been given to me, that's how sure I was that I had received an assignment from God to pray. We should pray for others and there are different types of intercessors with different prayer assignments. I met some of the godliest upright excellent people during those prayer meetings. You learn much about people going to prayer everyday with them. Some of things I've learned I want to teach to others so they can pray effectively and know how to use the different kinds of prayer. We need to teach others the things we have learned such as praying the scriptures, knowing the character of God etc.

If you are reading this book, I don't believe it is a coincidence. God is most likely going to use you in intercessory prayer. God is going to use what you have learned in you and you will teach others. You wouldn't want to read this book, or study on types of prayer if God wasn't calling you to a place of intercession. I know it has been a call on my life so strongly since I was first a Christian. There is a strong pull on me to pray for the blessing and benefit of others. There is a joy released when the people are healed or delivered or blessed.

Jehovah Rohi is Jehovah our shepherd. He leads me. Psalm 23. He leads me beside living waters. He leads me into green pastures. He is a God who loves me and cares for my soul. God can lead you and direct you. I don't mean in a vague way. I mean He can direct you the right way and you will feel peace. I heard Gloria Copeland say this "Let peace be your umpire". I like baseball so I understand the Umpire makes calls such as in or out or safe etc. The Holy Spirit is our Umpire. Gloria literally said if you are trying to make a decision but don't know the way – literally say to the Holy spirit " Holy Spirit I believe I am going to go in this direction… state the way you believe might be best.. and say – if its not the best way please correct me." Literally the Holy Spirit will either check you in your spirit or release you. O that has been so important to me in many decisions. The Holy Spirit will always correct us if we obey His prompting.

I am talking about major decision making such as should I marry this person? Should I take this job? Should I move? I'm not talking about praying over what brand of cereal you are going to buy. For the most part I make all my own decisions. I have education and experience. I believe God lets me choose what I want.
Making choices

I am talking about times we are not sure – which way to go. It usually involves other people; it is usually complex. God will let us choose but if you are not sure – that should be brought to God in the manner I've described. God will lead you with His peace. If you feel a check in your spirit, you should not proceed. Obey the promptings of the Holy Spirit. I've learned this by testimony but also by experience. God was so merciful to me. I was watching a TV show I had always watched but I felt a check like "don't watch this. It is no good for you. It's not right turn it off." I had never had an issue with this show in the past. It was something I always watched. Be obedient to the LORD to obey those promptings. Later I was begging God to have mercy on me and forgive me because of the way my spirit felt – like garbage had been dumped in there – unclean. Should you get a prompting from the Holy Spirit that says that is not the direction for you – you get that feeling? You obey. It could be the purchase of a car, or marrying a person or going to a place. Be sensitive. Let the Holy Spirit be your Peace Umpire.

I am not mentioning names for no reason. These people have impacted my life so tremendously that it has strengthened my Christian faith in the foundations of my being. If you hear names and you don't know who these people are, start searching the Internet and get some of their teachings. It will build your faith; it will teach you; you can learn things from mature saints who learned them from other faithful people. You don't have to learn the hard way – you can learn from others. You want spiritual help? You want to grow spiritually? These people I am mentioning will help you. That is why I am mentioning them, They don't pay me to mention names and I don't do it lightly. These people are proven ministers of God who live lives of integrity.

God knows you more than you know you. He knows you because He formed you and placed you in your mother's womb. He knows your character; He knows what will make you glad; He knows what you like because He created you to be that way.

25

Jehovah Jireh: Our Provider Genesis 22: 14

We thank Him for our daily bread; we should. He provides for us. I am not being religious; 2/3 of the people on earth do not have the luxury or quantity of things that we have in North America and Europe. We should thank God for supplying for us. I have never known hunger except on a fast. I know what it is like to go without food on purpose and feel hunger. There are people – even Christians in different countries who have known hunger and believe me they are thankful for their food.

We should thank God for what we have. Food, clothing, shelter, freedom of worship… I could go on and on about the blessings we in North America have been give. Keep in an attitude of gratitude. It will make it easy for you to get into prayer without ceasing.

Be thankful for the small things as well as the big things. God cared enough about me that He cared if I had the cup of coffee I wanted. We should thank God for new things,. Thanksgiving releases joy in your spirit and it releases blessings over your life. I want to always be thankful for what God has given me; I want to be in a posture of thanksgiving.

There is a Chagal painting of the Giver – it a picture of one hand clearly giving a bouquet of Beautiful coloured flowers to a second hand. That's God. He gives to us always, always, always.

The fact you have air in your lungs or you can walk or run or do something, is God's gift to us. In the present, God is giving you life right this moment. Don't take it for granted. Thank God for the small things. Thank God for the sunset being pretty. Cultivate a heart of thanksgiving, that you would be quick to be thankful.

The God who Prospers us

Jehovah Jireh supplies our needs, but it isn't only financial. Oh yes it is financial. I could share with you story after story of how He has supplied for me financially, making a way for me, putting people in my life who gave to me etc. Prosperity is more than just financial. He provides for us food, shelter, friends, family, opportunities.

God wants to prosper you financially. In the Old Covenant the book of Deuteronomy is dedicated to teaching the blessings of the LORD towards His people – with things. Jesus is the Messiah who has fulfilled all of the requirements of the Old Covenant. We are partakers of the blessings. Jesus, the new Adam, grafts us into His side. Jesus makes us heirs with Israel to bless us with all things we need. Read the blessings of Deuteronomy 28 over yourself. Pray them for yourself if you haven't already done so. He supplies for us in all areas of need.

He comforts us with a comfort that goes beyond anything of this earth. Upon the loss of my mother, God comforted me so much. I was so close to my mother. Once she became a born-again spirit filled Christian, she and I became the closest friends sharing the things of God together, praying together, reading the Bible together etc. I am so comforted knowing she is with the LORD. I am so thankful for the memories of her praying and praising and taking communion with me. God comforts me knowing she is with Him. God can supply you with comfort that surpasses all of earthly knowledge upon the loss of a loved one.

You might know that your loved one knew the LORD but it can comfort you this way. The mercy God showed towards you in drawing you to Himself and saving you from yourself and from destruction – that same mercy was reaching out to your loved one. If you were praying for them and others were, you know God was releasing chances for those people to come to Christ. They had up to the last second of their life on earth to make a decision for Christ. Let God's mercy be a comfort to you.

Jehovah Nissi – the LORD our banner –

Ex 17: 15 Then Moses built an altar and called the name of it, The LORD Is My Banner;

He is our deliverer; He is our victory. I know what it is like to be in bondage. I don't just mean before I was saved. Even when I was first a Christian I had some things that were bondages. We don't use that language too much anymore. We kind of cleaned up the language and say they were bad habits. Bondage is like what the slave traders do. They still exist. I don't know if you know it or not. They place iron shackles on the wrists and ankles of the slaves. Those people are lead and they have no choice about what they are doing or where they are going. They are in irons, led by an enemy, used and abused. They can't escape because of their bondages – those chains stop them from living a free life.

Bondages are sins you can't seem to get away from. They always tempt you and you fail repeatedly. I've known people who have quit smoking and kept going back to it; people who were in bondage to alcohol or drugs and kept going back to it. They are weaknesses, bad habits, sins. They have a hold on you just as sure as those irons have hold of the human slaves; these sins have a hold on you. You can't get free on your own.

Deliverance

Jehovah Nissi is our banner. He gives us victory. We used to sing a chorus " The Lion of Judah will break every chain and give to us the victory again and again." Do you know the Lion of Judah? He will break every chain. Just as sure as those iron chains can be broken with the right tools, Jesus can break those chains off you. This is what I mean. You wouldn't have to go to your 7 step programs any more. Please know I am not against 7 step programs. Every alcoholic and drug addict they help is a tremendous thing. What I am telling you is that you can be set free spiritually so that do not need any support – it will be as though it never existed. You won't want it. You won't be tempted by it. You won't even consider it. You will be fixed on Jesus and the freedom that He has given you to do whatever you want with your life.

Some people go for prayer – you receive your freedom but keep on going back into that sin. I am saying it can be broken off your life permanently. Let me share an example that the LORD gave me in a dream. I had thought I was doing well spiritually. I was following the LORD the best I could; I never missed a service; I was involved in the church. God gave me this dream. It is graphic so please receive a warning. I was at Church in the dream and there was a funeral. I stood by as they rolled the casket. I being too curious for my own good opened the lid to see who it was; to my horror it was me – a zombie me. It grabbed on to me and tried to pull me into that casket. It was vividly gross. I know it was a dream from God and God was showing me that I must not let the old sinful nature have any place in my life. I must start proclaiming I am the redeemed of Calvary rather than talking about the old life. You old life is gone – buried.with Christ in baptism. Don't dig up the coffin.

There is a whole realm in the Christian Church that has this particular flow; it has been infected by worldly psychology and theories of men. It teaches that a person must dig into the past to uncover things and release and talk about things of the past. They believe this will in some way pet the person's ego and by their self-pity will give them a feeling of special worth. Personally, I would like to see this whole realm of Christian counselling and social work run out of the Church completely because it is fleshly and promotes the things of the flesh. Instead of digging up the coffin and wasting your efforts on trying to revive the rotting corpse, accept your resurrection life in Christ. Proclaim Jesus victory over all your life and live it.

## Freedom through Jesus Christ

You can be totally set free by Jesus blood and His victory. It is all of Christ and none of you. You must receive it. You must believe it; you must live it. God's Word is the truth and we need to align with His Word. I don't know if you have ever seen a snake shedding its skin. It is quite fascinating. They are not my favourite animals, but to watch them pull themselves out of their old dead skin is fascinating. The dry, dead skin cells remain, but the animal pulls out of it and is renewed. God our deliverer, God our banner can set you free from bondages or sins that try to get hold of you. You can be set free from your past. Don't believe the lie that your past has to affect your future. No it doesn't. Your past does not determine your future. What you choose now in the present and the things you choose moment by moment affects your future.

I am talking about spiritually; I am talking about your soul (your mind, your will, your emotions). Digging up your past is not necessary to receive deliverance. You can go right to the deliverer. If you haven't repented – repent. Let Jesus wash you with His blood. Start praying and saying what God's Word says about you as a new creation in Christ. Let the Word of God be your foundation. Use Jesus Himself as your example.

Jesus can give you victory over all things – even genetics. You may say genetically it is not possible. Alcoholism runs in my family. You may believe that because your family is prone to a disease or bondage, you must also. It is a lie.

## Keep your mouth speaking in alignment with God

Some people talk themselves into an early grave. They say things like " my family dies young" so you yourself are speaking words to curse yourself. Start studying God's Word about how God wants you to live a long, healthy life. You also have to take care of the body you are using on earth by not feeding it garbage and giving it rest and exercises etc. You do not have to be bound by genetics. I am not letting my past, nor my genetics determine my future. You do not have to either. Jesus can give you new DNA. What? I mean Jesus was born of the Virgin Mary with no earthly father. His DNA is from God Himself. This same Jesus lives in you if you have been born again. Our heritage is from the line of Judah. Our heritage is from the first born from the dead. We are the inheritors of the promises of Abraham through Jesus Christ.

You must do your part. If all your family died obese, you could lose some weight. You could exercise. You could change from unhealthy habits to healthy ones. You are a son or daughter of the LORD; you should be living long and strong. You don't have to die from the diseases they died from. Oh yes there is something you can do. Do your part and pray for God to help you and receive His word as the highest authority in your life.

My Life Changed

When I turned 50, I made a major life decision because of some Christian preaching. Joyce Meyer testified that God had dealt with her about not carrying for her body with exercise. She has an excellent teaching on treating your body as a Temple of the Holy Spirit. She obeyed the LORD. It touched my heart because I knew I was not doing anything either; I received the word as a word for myself. She was saying how her husband had always done physical activity but she didn't until that day that God convicted her. She said God told her to care for the body she was living in or she would not finish strong in the last part of her life. Her telling her testimony on TV convicted me.

As if that wasn't enough, Gloria Copeland released a new book on Living Long: Finish Strong. She was talking about expecting to live long and taking care of your body and believing God's Word for long life. Gloria Copeland was saying you don't have to live the same life span of the others in your family. You can outlive them. She started saying we should start talking that we are going to live a long, healthy life.

I am saying you do not have to believe the lie that you have to be bound by your genetics. Even if it was a doctor or nurse who told you. You start doing something about caring for your body and get your words in alignment with Scripture. Start talking about yourself living a long life. Start listening to Christian Doctors. Read what they have to say about living long and strong. How can you increase your life span? How can you live as long as possible?

Some people, especially after the death of a loved one, wonder why they should go on living and don't see it as a priority. The truth is you should live because you are a Christian. Until Jesus comes, there are going to be people who need to get saved. You could be praying for people, witnessing to people, making a difference in the earth for the glory of God. Your life matters – you are salt and light in the earth. You are giving; you are caring; you can make a difference. Why not live long and strong to be 100 or 120? Why not disciple people and pray with people and impart things God has taught you to others? Aim high – go for the high call of God on your life. I know there is terrible loss after the loss of a loved one – but you can make a difference for Christ with your life. Start volunteering. Do what you can do.

Jehovah Adoni – He is our master. Let's never get away from the idea that God is our Master – our teacher. Ex 21: 6 There is a teaching in the Old testament that talks about if you have a slave and in the 7th year that you set him free – he loves you and chooses to serve you, you are to take an awl and pierce through his ear. This shows he freely chooses to serve you for the rest of his life. Some masters were good to their slaves and gave them food, shelter, money etc. If you haven't done so, please read the Old Testament of how you were supposed to treat the slaves. In the 7th year you had to set the slaves free, but some loved their masters so much they stayed by their own free will.

I made that decision when I was first a Christian. I realized Jesus had set me free. I had freedom to choose whatever I wanted. I had a new sense of freedom. In fact, I knew I didn't have to stay with the LORD. I could go and do anything – I could choose whatever life I wanted. I realized I had freedom. It was the first time in my life I felt free to do whatever I wanted. I said to the LORD I have seen you are good. You have given me freedom; it's your way I want. I chose Him for all my life. I got my ears pierced. I often think of it in connection with that scripture – not always but often. It's a reminder to me that even though I am free – I am choosing my life with God – moment by moment day after day for the rest of my life. I willingly choose to serve the LORD.

I am a willing servant of the LORD God Almighty; I choose to serve Him. I want to; it's my pleasure to do it.

God is my friend – the Holy Spirit my closest friend. I also remember God's majesty; He is sitting on a throne in heaven. Angels cover their faces because of the radiance of the glory that is on Him. Hosts of thousands of angels and saints are worshipping Him; He is LORD God almighty. Read chapter 7 Revelation about the glory of the LORD. There are thunders, lightning around the throne. Don't forget the grandeur of God. He has given you entrance by His blood into the Holy of Holies.

El Elyon – Psalm 91:1 He is the almighty, most high God. He is omnipotent. He lead Israel out of Egypt and literally divided the Red Sea so Israel could pass by on dry ground. He is a God of miracles and might.

El Shaddai – This is the last one I'll mention here. Gen 49: 25. He is all sufficient. He supplies more than what we need. Some religions have some gods who are higher than others. It is illogical to me. If there are some higher ones, why not just serve the higher ones? Why bother with the lower ones?

There is no higher God than Jehovah – He is the LORD of LORDS and King and Kings. There are no other real gods. Demons fool people into worshipping them. They were angels who sinned with the Devil. They were thrown out of heaven. They live in the atmospheres of the earth. People make idols to worship these false gods – believing the lie they are gods. We are forbidden to make idols. Don't pray to a picture of Jesus or a statue of Jesus – we are commanded to worship only the LORD.

Don't worship the cross. It was the way Jesus died but in itself it is not Holy or special. Jesus is the one we should be worshipping. Don't pray to your prayer beads – they are simply beads. If they help you to remember to pray good – but in themselves they are nothing but beads. Most Protestants may not agree with me. I'm not against using things to help us to pray, but if you worship those things themselves, it is wrong. If you are using prayer beads to pray and reading this book, ask the LORD out loud " Lord can I continue to use these beads or am I using them in some sort of idolatry?" Literally I believe God will speak to you. If He corrects you, obey Him.

I once had a friend who was convicted by God for praying to pictures of Jesus. They were nice pictures of Jesus but God convicted her and said don't pray to images. No one really knows what Jesus looks like. The closest thing we have is the Shroud of Turin if it is authentic. We are forbidden by the 2nd commandment not to make idols or pray to them. We pray to God Himself – we don't need a picture.

Jesus is our Saviour – be thankful He is your Saviour who saved you from sin, death and hell. He is mighty to save.

# 3 PRAYER: THANKSGIVING AND PRAISE

Knowing the different types of prayer, helps a believer to effectively use God's Word and also the type of prayer that would be most effective. Some people believe that prayer is anything that comes of out your mouth to God. Also there is some truth to it, God listens to sincere prayer and is merciful towards us, we can learn Biblical ways to pray effectively in different types of situations just as we can learn to use different equipment for different jobs or different equipment for different sports. This analogy is taken from Mary Alice Isleib's Book on Effective Fervent Prayer (1994). I would recommend it be taught in Bible colleges because it covers all different types of prayers a person would need to use.

Thanksgiving and Praise

Psalm 100: 4 Enter into His gates with thanksgiving,
and into His courts with praise;
be thankful to Him, and bless His name.
5 For the LORD is good; His mercy endures forever,
and His faithfulness to all generations.

God's Word instructs us how we should approach God and it is with thanksgiving and praise. We should be focused on God as our Creator and Saviour and LORD. First of all releasing thanksgiving encourages your own spirit. Also, it is the proper way to enter to speak with God who has given us all things. An attitude of thanksgiving places us in the right position to our LORD. I would compare thanksgiving as the outer court of the Lord in Solomon's Temple.

You can't get closer to God without being thankful. The priests could not get into the Holy place without going into the outer court. It was a place where you and I – Gentiles could go to pray. We could not go further. It was a place for priests to come and wash (foot laver and hand laver) and offer a sacrifice (blood from an animal). Jesus' blood made the way for us to be cleansed from all sin and unrighteousness. It is certainly a way of humility and recognizing God as our creator, protector and provider. Thankful should be a word that is used to describe us. People should notice that we Christians are thankful. It is unique because the tide of the world is to demand what is ours and to focus on ourselves and what we deserve. I am completely in favour of people's rights but I thank God Jesus took upon Himself on the cross when He died all that I deserve.

The Joy of Salvation

We should start thanking God for the joy of our salvation. If you think of how Jesus drew you to Himself like a magnet drawing metal pieces, if you remember His compassion on you when you didn't do things properly and He forgave you, if you remember the goodness of God towards you, most certainly you should be thankful. Where would you be had He not reached towards you in His mercy and love? A person who regularly remembers the joy of his or her salvation, will be a thankful person. You will have the same first joy that you had when you gave your life to God. That first love – joy will cause you to view life from a different perspective. We will be thankful for large things and thankful for small things. There is nothing that is too big to thank God for or too small to thank God for. This thankfulness will also be shown towards people. It will make us notable.

Praising God with All Your Being

Thanksgiving should be one of our character qualities and it is the first way we draw closer to God. Praise is the next aspect. You start thanking God for your salvation, for forgiving you, for providing for you, for healing you…etc. make it personal. Upon thanking God, you will become so overwhelmed with thanksgiving, you are going to start praising Him. The praise is acknowledging God for who He is – His character qualities, His Word, His blessings, His unique love for you personally.

Oh the praising is easy if you focus on how awesome God is and what He has done for you, what He has done for others etc. Start praising God for answering your prayers even before you see the answers in the natural. If you know He has heard your prayer, you know you have the petitions you have asked of Him. That is something to praise God for. This could be described as the Holy Place in the Temple of Solomon. It was a place where priests offered incense. It was a place closer to God's presence. Not everyone could go into in this place because it was consecrated for certain priests to offer praise. It was a place of focus direct on praising God. Jesus' blood gives us entrance into the Holy Place – Our praises are as an offering giving glory to God.

A person who regularly praises God is going to overflow with joy. In God's presence is Joy. It will influence us in our relationships. It will influence us in our outlook. It will influence us in how we treat others. We will be kind. We will want others to have the joy of the LORD. We will want to speak words of encouragement to others. We will be given to being positive knowing that God is with us.

1 Corinthians 6 : 19 What? Do you not know that your body is the temple of the Holy Spirit, who is in you, whom you have received from God, and that you are not your own? 20 You were bought with a price. Therefore, glorify God in your body and in your spirit, which are God's.

God the Holy Spirit lives in you. You are the dwelling place of the Holy Spirit of God. We should be praising and praying throughout our day communing with God. The awesome thing about being a Christian is that we are the dwelling place where God lives. We are not on a quest to find God. We are not on a journey to find God. He came to us and revealed Himself to us. He lives in us and we live in Him. We are His body on the earth. God lives in us.

The Most Holy Place

The most Holy place in the Temple of Solomon was the Holy of Holies. It was the innermost chamber that had the Ark of the covenant in it. The mercy seat on the ark was covered by two angels whose wings spread over it. It was the place of atonement. This was the most Holy place. There was a thick curtain dividing the Holy place from the Most Holy Place. Only the High priest, once a year could enter in to offer sacrifice for the atonement of the people of Israel. He has a rope around his foot with bells on it. This place was so Holy, that if there was any sin at all, the person would die. The rope was there because if the high priest didn`t come out and they stopped hearing the bells, the people would pull him out. No one dared to enter in in to this most Holy place. God`s manifest presence would be so strong in that place that when Moses and Aaron would enter in (to the Tabernacle in the wilderness the first home for the Ark) a glory cloud would form over the tabernacle.

Exodus 40: 34 Then the cloud covered the tent of meeting, and the glory of the LORD filled the tabernacle. 35 Moses was not able to enter into the tent of meeting because the cloud settled on it, and the glory of the LORD filled the tabernacle.

Jesus` death burial and resurrection paid the price for us and made us as kings and priests to our God. After he died on the cross, the veil or curtain in the Temple was torn from the top down. Please understand the significance. It was not torn by any human. From the top down, God made a way for us to enter the Holy of Holies. God has made the way for us to enter with boldness before His throne of mercy.

Revelation 1: 5 and from Jesus Christ, who is the faithful witness, the firstborn from the dead, and the ruler of the kings of the earth. To Him who loved us and washed us from our sins in His own blood, 6 and has made us kings and priests to His God and Father, to Him be glory and dominion forever and ever. Amen.

The Holy of Holies

It is a place or worship and communion with God – oneness – wholeness. It is a place where God`s presence is so strong that it overwhelms you. It is the type of glory that a human eye cannot see. It can only be viewed as we worship in spirit and truth. Worshippers are enthralled with the presence of God. Worshippers are not making petitions here. They are abandoned to worship and meditate on the beauty and glory of God. This type of manifold beauty can only be seen in the spirit. You think of how magnificent God is and suddenly a new though of God`s magnificence comes.

The New Ark of the Covenant

The presence of God was in the ark of the covenant in the Old Testament. Jesus made the way for us to enter the Holiest of all, also His Holy presence lives in us – you are the Ark of the Covenant. You are the dwelling place of the highest God. The book of Hebrews shows us there is a real Temple in heaven where God is seated. There is the most Holy place. The things of the earth are types of the heavenly. Jesus poured His own blood on that mercy seat to cleanse us from all sin – all people past, present, future; His blood made atonement for them.

Jesus, the Lamb of God gave Himself for us so that we might have direct access to God. We can approach the throne with boldness knowing it is Jesus` blood that covers us and not our own righteousness, which is as filthy rags. Jesus blood not only covers our sin; it erases our sin. It releases us from bondage and gives us freedom to choose God. Jesus sits in the throne room interceding for us. He is praying for us.

Hebrews 7: 25 Therefore He is able to save to the uttermost those who come to God through Him, because He at all times lives to make intercession for them.

Jesus, our high priest is interceding for you. You are praying; He is in the Holiest place of all praying for you. His blood makes you holy. His blood gives you entrance as a priest and king. Jesus is your best prayer partner. Come into agreement with the Word of God and you`ll be in agreement with God`s will. His Word explains His will for all people on Earth.

I have heard teaching that says the Old Testament is really filled with types and shadows of the New Testament, and there is truth to it but the Old Testament is not only a type and shadow of the New Testament, it is also a reflection of Heaven. The commandments given to Moses apply to us today. The whole Bible is complete as God`s Word. Some people think you don`t need the Old Testament. Jesus fulfilled all of the Levitical laws of the Old Testament. He fulfilled all the Messianic prophecies of the Old Testament. The New Covenant is a fulfillment of God`s promise to us.

Starting your Prayer Life

It may be new to you. Don`t try to start like a giant. Don`t aim too high. Aim for a commitment you can keep. Yonggi Cho, International House of Prayer, others who fast and pray and give themselves to a life of prayer are admirable. We should respect and admire them. But think of it like the Olympics. You don`t join the Olympics and become a champion without a life of training. Athletes who aim for excellence practice. They give time and effort to discipline themselves to become excellent at their sport. I make the analogy to prayer. You want to give yourself something you can do to start.

Starting A Prayer Life

If you are new or you want to try a new way of prayer, set aside 15 minutes. I would recommend starting by giving several of those minutes to thanking God for your salvation, for blessing you and providing for you. Start praising God for how good He has been to you. Thank Him for your blessing of the present day.

I would suggest you make a list of your petitions or things you are asking God for including your loved ones and others you want to prayer for. You could literally time yourself.

Pray about those requests and spend the last 4 to 6 minutes thanking God and praising Him for answering your prayers even before you physically see it — receive it with your spirit. If you do not know what to do to praise, get the words to some of the hymns and songs that you sing at church and start singing them. Be sure to also personalize the praise by thanking God for what He has personally done for you. This is a form of the new song of the Lord that magnifies God and gives Him your personal best praise. If you do not know any Christian praise and worship songs start by speaking with the worship leader at your church. Listen to Christian radio or satellite or Internet radio. Christian music includes jazz, rock, country etc.

You may feel hesitant to sing or believe your voice isn't very good. Get alone and praise. You are singing to God. I remember a nice young man who was a worship leader and we had been in a camp meeting atmosphere and there was much praise and worship and it was quite long. He confessed that is voice was weak and sounded funny not like normal because he had been singing so much. The Lord had given him a revelation when he said that he couldn't do his normal but he would give God the best He could even with a hoarse throat — but God told him to give his best, that is what requires of us. God said to Him it sounded beautiful because it was sincere worship.

An excellent book that goes into much more detail than this would be Growing In Prayer by Mike Bickle. I highly recommend this book as it gives in depth practical teaching to people who want to learn to press in to God in prayer.

Make Time for Prayer

It is not good enough to pray only at church. It is not good enough to read the Bible only at church. It is not good to only praise at church. It is right to do it at church but we need it every day of our lives not only on church days. It should be a habit of a born again Christian to have a relationship with God — that includes reading the Bible, praying and praising at home. If you have to fit it in your schedule — set a timer for 15 minutes. I have been in prayer meetings where there is literally a timer and so many minutes are spent in individual prayer and so many hours are spent in corporate prayer.

You can get prayer into your schedule if you set a timer and plan to give yourself to prayer during that period. You can learn the different types of prayer and use them as you pray for different things.

Ephesians 6: 18 Pray in the Spirit always with all kinds of prayer and supplication. To that end be alert with all perseverance and supplication for all the saints.

You, a born-again – spirit-filled Christian are a House of Prayer – You are the Temple of the Lord. He lives in you. Christians are the living stones of Temple of the Holy Spirit on the earth. The Holy Spirit of the living God lives inside of you. Are you pleasing to Him? Wherever you go, you bring the LORD; whatever you do, you bring the Lord with you. Keep your vessel with Holiness. It is so important that we respect the presence of God and not take it for granted. If you would offer yourself to God – saying `God, I give myself to you – use me this day each day``, God would commune with you more. You could give yourself to speaking to God and listening to God speak to you throughout your day.

You must be without unconfessed sin to speak with God. God hates sin. He is repulsed by it.

1 Thessalonians 5: 19 Do not quench the Spirit.

Your life should be such that if you sin, you repent immediately. If you truly do love God, you will not want to grieve the Holy Spirit. You will not be trying to sin; you will do anything you can to live your life pleasing to God. Grieving the spirit means the Holy Spirit is offended. You will know if this is true because you will it inside you. Sin separates you from God. Please, should this happen, run to God. Turn to Him and ask Jesus to forgive you. He will. His blood was once and for all.

1 John 1: 9 If we confess our sins, He is faithful and just to forgive us our sins and cleanse us from all unrighteousness.

There are consequences to sin. If you do not repent, you are likely to plunge deeper into sin. The enemy of your soul will try to trap you into bondages to sin. The demons that hate you will be able to snare you because you have stepped outside of God`s protection. There is a special protection of covering over a Christian who is living godly. It is a place of freedom and rejoicing, It is dangerous to hold onto sin. It always has a price.

Romans 6:23 For the wages of sin is death, but the gift of God is eternal life through Jesus Christ our Lord.

There is no exception – sin always ends in death. It starts with spiritual death and bondage to sin and could also lead to all that the world has to offer in terms of sin and hell and death. As Moses lead Israel through the wilderness, the people sinned by making a golden calf; others sinned by blaming Moses for taking them away from their leeks and onions in Egypt.

They were ungrateful. They accused Moses of making Himself their leader – Moses said if they were guilty in their false accusation against him that the earth would swallow them up – right after that, the earth opened up and some of these people were judged for their sin immediately as the earth swallowed them.

Holiness - What if you did not repent and today was your last day? Are you right with God? Holiness is essential for prayer. Only Jesus blood gives us this holiness. We must stay right with God to keep our boldness to approach His throne. If you are not right with God, the only prayer you can pray is a repentance prayer. Do it. Repent quickly. Please know God is merciful. There is nothing that you have done that is a surprise to God. He knew about it the day he died on the cross; He paid your debt in full that day.

You will not worship any other God. You will not make idols. You will not lie. You will not covet. You will keep God as the Lord of the Sabbath. You will not kill or hate. You will not steal. You will honour your parents. You will not abuse the name of God (swear). You will not commit adultery.

You say – it is hard to keep the commandments. I tell you it is impossible to keep the commandments in your own strength. If you live in the spirit, if you live in communion with God – the Holy Spirit who lives in you will empower you to live a Holy life. Don't believe the lie that you have to live in sin. Jesus set us free from the curse of the law. Part of that curse was being in our own strength and failing repeatedly. That`s why they had to offer blood sacrifices to cover their sin.

Jesus paid the price not only to forgive your sin but to free you from sin nature. You can live in Holiness because of Jesus blood. The Holy Spirit living in you and through you can help you to do all things in righteousness. You can live a Holy life. God said "Be ye holy as I am holy"( 1 Peter 1:16) , It doesn`t mean you might never – it means it should not be a normal part of a Christian`s life. Life in the Spirit is living by the Holy Spirit of God who lives in you and through you.

In the 1990's Larry Lea had some tremendous books. He had an awesome book called: Can you not tarry with me one hour?" It is a book about prayer. I want to highly recommend that book if you are a new Christian or you want to get in to a deeper prayer life. I didn't know there were deeper depths of prayer. Haven't you found that the more you learn about Jesus, the more there is to learn about Him? The more I get to know Him, the more I get to love Him. I more I learn, the more I realize there is much more I need to learn. There are pleasures in God. There is pleasure in knowing Him and Him revealing Himself to us through His Word.

International House of Prayer

I love what Mike Bickle says and that is it is a lie that prayer is boring. If you have not heard any teaching from International House of prayer Kansas City, I highly recommend you get teaching on prayer. The Church is dedicated 24/7 to prayer and praise. They have a live web stream and they also have an on demand web stream of various prayer rooms. Always at that Church someone is praying, praising, interceding. The praise and worship music is awesome but it is because the people have given themselves to worshipping God. They are wholly given to God. I would say they have been one of the biggest influences on my spiritual life over this past near decade; certainly, I have learned much from them on prayer and worship and living consecrated to God. Some teachings can change your life forever.

Intimacy with God

You can grow in the knowledge of spiritual things line upon line, precept upon precept, bit by bit by bit but suddenly a teaching can come that can propel you to a higher level. There are new opportunities, new outlook, new vision, new ideas – a whole new realm. God is the most intimate relationship you can have. If your earthly relationships with family are important – your spiritual relationship with God should be as well. He is a person. He is fascinating. He knows everything about you. He is dynamic. The relationship with God grows as we draw close and He reveals more and more of Himself to us. You alone can decide how much time you should give in prayer but you should be growing. Your relationship with God should not be stale.

If He is not the most fascinating person to you, start praying the scriptures to God. Literally start reading the Psalms out loud to God with passion. They are almost all praise and worship to God for the awesome things He has done and of course for who He is. As we pray God's Word (I will teach on it later) to Him, we will hear the Word of God and it will release faith in our spirits. If you have said you would pray for someone, do it. Write it in a place to remind you or if possible do it right there at that moment so you won't forget.

Make a list

It is good to make a list of people and things to pray for. You do not have to follow the list completely every day, but it gives you a good guideline to go by. Something important to pray for your own self is wisdom. Ask God to give you wisdom in decision making. Pray for God to give you wisdom in your job, in your family, in your friendships etc. Pray for those in authority in your life. Pray for your company, for your boss; pray for the people you see every day or occasionally. Pray for what they have need of. What do they need?

Prayer is for all Areas of Your Life

There is no area of your life that you shouldn't praying about. All parts of your life should be matters of prayer. Pray for your Church, your pastors, the members you know, the members you don't know. These people pray for us, we should be praying for them. Especially pray for the Apostles, the prophets, the pastors, the teachers, the evangelists. These people impart the living word of God to you; we should be praying for them. Add them to your prayer list.

Make a Plan.

You may use it all or parts of it. You will find you will constantly add to it and be updating it. Pray for yourself and pray for others. I am not even talking about deep intercessory prayer yet. Pray for others the perfect will of God for them. I don't know anyone who doesn't know somebody who needs salvation. You can categorize your prayer list into Salvation, Healing, Deliverance, physical or financial needs etc. It depends on how detailed you want to get. The person you may know that is unsaved, what if you are the only person who knows Christ in his or her life? Do you realize you might be the only person who would pray for that person? As we pray for others, God softens their hearts and gives them opportunities to receive Him as Saviour and Lord.

Pray for Yourself

For yourself wisdom, knowledge and discernment are very important. These giftings released in your life could mean choosing a right way rather than the wrong one. Spiritual discernment helps you to know the way to go. You can know the situation you are in by discernment. Pray for the gifts of the Spirit. Stir up the gifts of the Spirit. Pray that God would grow you in the fruit of the Spirit. You are the planting of the LORD, a tree of righteousness. Pray that you will bear much fruit for God. People will see your life and they will see peace, joy, forbearance, love etc. Live excellently so people will wonder about the reason for the hope that is in you.

1 Corinthians 12: 7 But the manifestation of the Spirit is given to everyone for the common good. 8 To one is given by the Spirit the word of wisdom, to another the word of knowledge by the same Spirit, 9 to another faith by the same Spirit, to another gifts of healings by the same Spirit, 10 to another the working of miracles, to another prophecy, to another discerning of spirits, to another various kinds of tongues, and to another the interpretation of tongues. 11 But that one and very same Spirit works all these, dividing to each one individually as He will.

Galatians 5: 22 But the fruit of the Spirit is love, joy, peace, patience, gentleness, goodness, faith, 23 meekness, and self-control; against such there is no law.

Ask for Your Own Needs

Never be ashamed to ask about your own needs such a job or a car or what it is you most need. Yonggi Cho was a profound influence on my life concerning prayer. His book on the 5th dimension in God is excellent. God taught him to be so specific in prayer that when he prayed for a bicycle – God asked him what colour and what style. God wants us to be specific in our prayer requests. Never think it isn't important to ask about your own needs. God cares. In fact, He cares that you get what you want so be specific.

Pray for God's Will

I wish I could say it was at the beginning of my life serving God but it wasn't; it was several years into serving Him, I noticed all my prayers were going one way. I was praying for me, for my friends, for my church, for my loved ones etc. It was all about me. At one point, it came to me; I actually want to know God's heart – what He wants me to pray for. I started praying asking God to reveal His heart to me so I could pray in agreement with Him. I started praying to have the heart that God has for things important to God; I wanted to love the Church the way God loves the Church. I started asking God to help me to pray for people with His heart for them – his love for them. I started to notice how God cares about all the people in all the countries of the world; I prayed that I might have God's heart for them.

If you begin asking God to help you to pray for things that He cares about, He will answer you. You will start to notice people you never noticed before. You will care about people you pass by on the street. You may start noticing that God will use you throughout the day to pray over people you don't even know, but God will tug at your heart. It could be a person; it could be an animal. I know I lost some people right there but it is true; sometimes,

God inspires me to pray for animals. God cares about animals. He provides for them and most often He uses people to do it.

God's Heart

If you don't want to have God's heart, don't ask for it. If you don't want God to be your best friend, you don't have to have Him as your best friend. You determine how much of God you want in your life. God is willing that we should all come to Him intimately, but if you are not willing, He will never force you. You could stay in the Holy Place (in the Temple) or in a pretty close friendship with God and be saved. I am not talking about salvation. I am talking about intimacy with God. God wants to reveal His heart to you. Do you want to go deeper in God? I know some people who want to live in the Holy place. They are happy to have so much God in their lives and they love God but they want to stop at friends. They do not want intimacy.

There are some people who live between the Holy place and the outer court. They like to play with sin. They want to get as close to that outer court that they can. They want God in part of their lives but they want most of their lives to themselves. They are not interested in pressing into the Holy Place and staying there. There is a part of your life given to God. Almost always you are living for God. Not always just almost always. It isn't that you do away with God totally, you just put Him on the side and prioritize other things more. You can still be saved and live in the Holy place.

There are others who ride the line of the outer court and the gates of hell. They want to know how much sin they can get away with and still be able to jump back into the outer court and get cleansed. Some people determine that they will enjoy the pleasures of sin while they live, and at the last moment of their lives jump into the outer court and get clean. After all, Jesus Blood was shed once and for all. Yes; it is true - it is free and it is once and for all but it isn't cheap. Jesus life given for us is precious. If you don't accept it as precious, you should examine why it is you are a Christian at all. Jesus Christ is the center of our faith.

Communion with God

I am talking about all people. This is not only for fivefold ministry only. It applies to plumbers, carpenters, truck drivers, athletes any job possible. You can be doing your secular job and keep in communion with God. Do you thank God you could do your job today? Do you rely on Him to help you throughout the day? You can pray without ceasing. This is an attitude and posture of the heart. You give yourself to God each day and ask for His inspiration throughout the day. It is constant communion with God. You ask Him to help you; you thank Him for helping you; you pray for wisdom etc. You can commune with God constantly.

1 Thessalonians 5: 16 Rejoice always. 17 Pray without ceasing.

There is an invitation from God to come into intimate relationship with God in the Holy of Holies. You do not have to do it; you can choose the Holy place of friendship and occasional intimacy; you can choose the outer court with occasional praise and worship in the Holy place. Only you determine how much of God that you want. You never shut off God though. I am saying He is with you whether or not you are paying attention to Him. Are you glad that God is with you every place you go and whatever you are doing? There should be no part of our lives we should not want God a part of.

You have the Holy Spirit residing on the inside of you 24/7. Start including God in all parts of your life. Ask for wisdom; pray for understanding. Know that God wants to live with you helping you throughout your day. We were born to have intimate fellowship with God. We should never get so we believe we don't need to learn more about prayer or more about God.

I am not trying to impose legalism on you. You choose as close to God as you want to be; if you chose this book on prayer, you must be wanting more of God and more about prayer.

Baptism in the Holy Spirit – If you are not baptized in the Holy Spirit, you should be. You can be. Ask God to baptize you in the Holy Spirit. You don't have to have it to get to heaven but if you don't, you will never have the pleasure of having it; you would have the benefits of having it. The baptism of the Holy spirit is to empower us for service. God is higher, wider, greater, above, beyond, beneath – more awesome in all possible ways than you could ever ask or know.

# 4 PRAYING WITH UNDERSTANDING
# PRAYING THE ARMOR OF GOD
# PRAYING THE PRAYER OF PETITION

Praying with understanding means praying in the natural language that you speak. It means that you are not praying in the Holy Spirit speaking with other tongues. This teaching will focus on how to get an answer to your prayer. First, you should get dressed to pray. I take the Word literally. I pray each piece of armor on me. I thank God for the armor of God each day.

Ephesians 6: 11 Put on the whole armor of God that you may be able to stand against the schemes of the devil. 12 For our fight is not against flesh and blood, but against principalities, against powers, against the rulers of the darkness of this world, and against spiritual forces of evil in the heavenly places. 13 Therefore take up the whole armor of God that you may be able to resist in the evil day, and having done all, to stand. 14 Stand therefore, having your waist girded with truth, having put on the breastplate of righteousness, 15 having your feet fitted with the readiness of the gospel of peace, 16 and above all, taking the shield of faith, with which you will be able to extinguish all the fiery arrows of the evil one. 17 Take the helmet of salvation and the sword of the Spirit, which is the word of God.

This is the Apostle Paul teaching us how to prepare ourselves to do spiritual ware fare. In a sense, all prayer is advancing the kingdom of God as we pray for His will to be done on earth as it is in heaven.
Spiritual armour

I know that the armour of God is a spiritual analogy – but it is more than that. It is spiritual armour. The protection and covering is real. The shield of faith is real. The sword of the spirit is strong. Over twenty years ago, I was praying on a special prayer assignment with some people for a miracle – for my Pastor to live. We gathered daily. I was praying the armour of God over myself because I knew it was a battle. We were not praying for God to change. We knew that it was God's will for my Pastor to be healthy and strong. We knew we were fighting against evil forces that tried to kill him. That's when I started praying the armour of God on myself so strong.

One day, at church I started seeing armour on people. I know it sounds weird but it was true. It wasn't physical. It wasn't as though I believed they had on physical armour. I could see it was spiritual. I could see some people didn't have on the breastplate of righteousness. I could see others were missing pieces of armour or had it on wrong etc. What this did is it cause me to pray for those people specifically about their spiritual armour. I knew that it represented more than just spiritual clothing but also aspects of their lives that needed to be strengthened. God can kind of give you spiritual insight by giving you a vision so that you can effectively pray

Here is an example given from Google Images (April 2016).

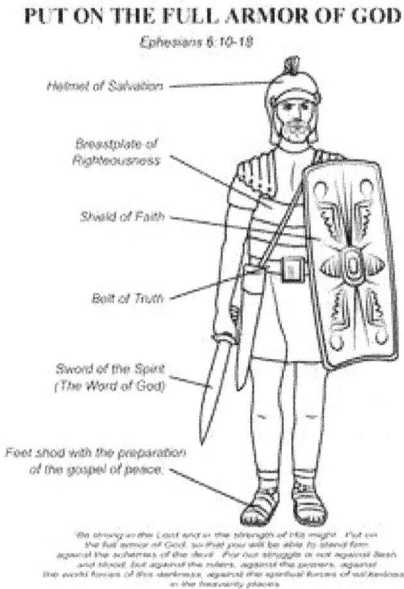

**PUT ON THE FULL ARMOR OF GOD**
Ephesians 6:10-18

Helmet of Salvation
Breastplate of Righteousness
Shield of Faith
Belt of Truth
Sword of the Spirit (The Word of God)
Feet shod with the preparation of the gospel of peace.

The Apostle Paul would have been familiar with Roman armor, similar to this. As a soldier wore armor to protect him, if we clothe ourselves with the armor of God, we will be able to stand against anything. I want you to think of standing as being unmovable. The Soldiers had a spike on their sandal to help them plant themselves firmly on the ground as they fought. It is this same type of standing that Paul encourages us to have. Being strong, being mighty is a result of putting on the armor of God. By praying the armor of God, I am reminding myself of God's protection but also the spirit realm. I am taking hold of what God has provided for us in His Word.

"having your waist girded with truth," This covers your waist and your private parts. The most vulnerable area is covered. First let me say, keep pure sexually. Be truthful to be covered with strength. Truth is the strongest force you could have there. It is standing in the righteousness of Jesus Christ.

" 15 having your feet fitted with the readiness of the gospel of peace," What this means is being a peace maker not someone who is given to strife. You don't have to live in strife. There are excellent teachings on this subject. I want to give you a couple of names – John Bevere has an excellent book titled "The Bait of Satan" and Joyce Meyer has a book titled "Life without Strife" (it has a new name but I am not sure of it). These books teach how the enemy – the devil uses people who are Christians as they live in their flesh and speak words to others that cause offence, hatred, gossip, etc. Strife should be avoided. You do not have to argue or be offended. You can choose to live beyond it.

"16 and above all, taking the shield of faith, with which you will be able to extinguish all the fiery arrows of the evil one."

Next the shield of faith. Faith is a mighty weapon. First of all it is our defense. If the enemy is shooting at us, we are protected by the shield. Give no place to the devil. We should have no spot on us not covered by the shield. It was huge. It covered the soldier. It was sometimes soaked in water so it fiery arrows were shot – it would extinguish them. Staying in the spirit – keeps you out of the flesh. Living in the faith realm of the Spirit, keeps you out of the flesh. You are supposed to live in the Spirit. You are to command your soul from the spirit. You are to live in the Spirit.

Without faith, it is impossible to please God. By faith are we saved through Jesus Christ. Faith is a top priority in the kingdom of God. Living by faith is using the shield of faith as a daily thing to protect you. Living by faith is believing in Jesus and living by the standard of the Word. It is a shield. It protects you. You've got to build up your faith with the Word of God, by praising, by praying, by speaking scripture to yourself.

Hebrews 11: 6 And without faith it is impossible to please God, for he who comes to God must believe that He exists and that He is a rewarder of those who diligently seek Him.

Ephesians 6: 17 Take the helmet of salvation and the sword of the Spirit, which is the word of God.

Without salvation, we have nothing. Our confidence comes from knowing Jesus blood has cleansed us. Our boldness comes from knowing our Saviour died and rose again. It is our salvation alone that gives us any place to stand against the enemy. Jesus victory is what we fight with. It is by Jesus' righteousness; it is by Jesus' holiness; it is by Jesus sitting on the Throne in gloy that we have confidence to proclaim His Word from the earth. It would be good to thank God each day for saving you. It will not only be thanksgiving to God but will give you boldness.

If a brother or sister in Christ offends you, you should go to that person and tell him or her. Often people are offended and the person who is responsible might not even know about it. Should you go to him or her, it may be resolved right there.

Matthew 18: 15 "Now if your brother sins against you, go and tell him his fault between you and him alone. If he listens to you, you have gained your brother. If the person does not repent, you are to bring a witness with you and approach the person again.

Strife comes in the flesh. It is arrogant; it is proud; it is haughty; it is self-righteous; it is hatred; it is the opposite of the type of love talked about in 1 Corinthians 13. There are unsaved people who live their lives in this way. They are not Christians; you can't expect them to know differently. This aught not be true of a Christian. A Christian should have the character of Christ. The fruit of the Holy Spirit should be evident in our lives.

1 Corinthians 13: 4 Love suffers long and is kind; love envies not; love flaunts not itself and is not puffed up, 5 does not behave itself improperly, seeks not its own, is not easily provoked, thinks no evil; 6 rejoices not in iniquity, but rejoices in the truth; 7 bears all things, believes all things, hopes all things, and endures all things.

Galatians 5: 22 But the fruit of the Spirit is love, joy, peace, patience, gentleness, goodness, faith, 23 meekness, and self-control; against such there is no law.

Godly character can only be developed by communing with God. A person who is gruff or ready to argue or accusing or any of these fleshly reasons people cause or get offended is not living a Christian life. This person may curse or say bad things. This is a person with an un renewed mind. These types of people grumble and complain and really have no idea of peace. It is a sinful condition that exists in a person's flesh or soulish nature. You do not have to stay that way. You can be renewed. You can memorize scripture until it is engrafted into your soul. The Word of God can give you a new nature. You can become a peace maker instead of a brawler

Standing in long lines can often bring out the worst in some people; they may be impatient or insulting or complaining etc. We should not be close friends with these types of people. You can pray for them but unless they are willing to change, don't let them get in your life; they will infect your life with poison.

Knowing the peace of Jesus Christ is a pleasure we Christians have but don't always thank God for. If you were someone who was in strife but now you are in peace – you will notice the difference. Jesus is the Prince of Peace. Let Him rule and obey the Holy Sprit's promptings to rephrase or repent or apologize etc. You will stay out of strife.

Cutting Strife off at the head

There are some people who will start strife in this way; they will say "This is not gossip but… so and so really said this about you…it was nasty …but I thought you should know…" They are trying to sow strife into you to cause you to be offended. Maybe the person took the comment out of context; maybe the person twisted it; maybe the person misunderstood. What you need to do is cut it off right there.

Instead of getting offended, determine to resolve it. State" Let's go see so and so…: If you suggest that you both go talk to the person about it right there, that will usually resolve it. Either the person will back out or the mentioned person will apologize.

The other thing you could do is say " Let's pray for the person. Pray rejecting those words and plead the blood over it so it will be stopped right there." Often, a spiritual response will end the situation. A person who want to stir up strife wants to run from prayer.

Let God Defend you

I know it is hard to believe there are Christians who do this, but if you have been in any type of close Christian fellowship, you will know that these types of situations arise and living in the flesh is the reason for it. The only way out of it is for someone to live above it in the spirit. You can take the approach of Matthew 18 to approach the person or you can take the approach of forgiving. I had a teacher who was very wise. Even though people said nasty things about him, he would examine himself to see if there was any truth to it at all. He was not offended and asked God to help him stay pure. His humble, non-offensive spirit is part of what has made him the mighty man of God he is today.

Pray to be a Peace Maker

If you see two Christians fighting, you should pray for wisdom on what to speak. An example of this can be seen in the New Testament Early Christian Church. There was some strife between Paul and Peter. Paul was ministering to Gentiles and preaching that circumcision was not necessary; that Gentiles could accept Christ without becoming Jews. Peter had been given Divine revelation on the topic and was seeing Gentiles come to Christ also. Peter, met up with Paul and was eating and drinking with the Gentile Christians but as soon as the Jewish Christians from Jerusalem came, he started keeping the Levitical laws; he was being a hypocrite. Paul accuses him of it openly and not kindly.

Thank God for James who was the head of the Jerusalem Church. He prayed and with wisdom spoke that the Gentiles need not become Christians but only abstain from blood or strangled animals. This was a word of wisdom directly solving the issue. If you are praying God help me be a peace- maker, God will give you the wisdom.

Joy of Salvation

As Christians, we should thank God regularly for saving us. There is much joy in your salvation, in knowing that you are forgiven, in knowing that you are in communion with God. It should release joy in us as we think about it. I realize there are all sorts of testimonies of have people come to Christ. Some people are born into Christian families and learn about God from Church and at home.

I thank God that even though I did not have a Christian family or go to church, God found a way to draw me to Himself so that I could know Him as Saviour and LORD. I know that I know it was miraculous Divine intervention that saved me from sin, hell, death, from my own iniquities, from my own sins, especially from my own sinful soul. It ought to release joy in you as you think about what God has done for you.

Even if our salvation only meant that after this life, we get to be with Jesus for eternity, that would be enough to be thankful for. But that is not all there is. By accepting Jesus as your Saviour, you enter eternity. You can start enjoying abundant life for the rest of your life. You can have life on earth that is extremely prosperous, healthy, strong, fruitful, effective and fulfilling.

If salvation were only to benefit us after death – God should just let us die as soon as we are saved. Being born again is not for the future only; it is for the present. It is for every area of our lives. What it gives us is a heavenly advantage in all areas of life on the earth. Of course part of it is that we want to share Christ with as many people as possible because we care that others receive life. Salvation affects every aspect of a human life – including work or career, family, friendships, associations etc.

Sword of the Spirit

The scripture compares the Word of God to a powerful sword. As a sword was used in battles, so we are to use the word of God in our situations. Whether it is an ordinary day where we pray the Word of God over ourselves for protection and blessing and favour or whether it is a tough spot or difficulty that we do not understand, God's Word is to be confessed, to be prayed and to be applied by faith to our lives.

Romans 10: 17
17 Consequently, faith comes from hearing the message, and the message is heard through the word about Christ.

As we speak God's Word to ourselves out loud, as we pray and apply the Word to our lives. Faith is ignited in our hearts to believe the Word. The Word of God has within itself the power to bring itself to come to pass. It is the inspired Word of God that was written by the Holy Spirit and that is interpreted by the Holy Spirit. It is God's will about matters of the earth. Confessing the Word of God out loud, praying it and applying it personally to our lives gives us faith and faith can move mountains.

As we pray for God to change situations, faith becomes increasingly more important. Whatever is not of faith is sin. If we want to pray effectively, we should align our prayers with what God has to say about the thing we are praying about. There are many books available that organize scripture by topic so we can apply them to life situations. I highly recommend you invest in some of these. Even though you could use the Internet to search by topic – I do believe there is a value in holding it in your hands and reading and praying those scriptures. You can create your own reference of scriptures.

I have several boxes of scriptures written on index cards that I believe God has quickened to me. I use them for prayer for myself and others. Literally praying the scripture aligns us completely with what God says about a matter. Personalizing the scriptures to your specific season or present reality will only help you to build up yourself in the faith. It is a skillful way of applying God's Word in prayer to your own life.

Knowing the Word of God is essential to your prayer life. The more scripture you know, the more scripture you can apply in your prayers. The more you read it, confess it and pray it in faith, the more it is engrafted into your soul. The scripture uses that analogy and it is a good one. I am a gardener and I have had several successful grafting experiences.

Grafted

It literally means taking a branch or growing part and joining it to a different plant or bush. It is done by making a V shaped cut into the part you want to graft with a corresponding cut into the new part. Example a male part and a female part. The two pieces should fit together like a puzzle. Sometimes, you can apply growing solution. I have used spittle. You wrap the two parts together with strong tape. The miracle of God's creation occurs as the parts of the branch grafted in joins with the branch it is grafted into. The two parts become one. The tree or plant becomes complete.

I thank God for the scriptures God has quickened to me and that I have prayed and confessed and believed in so that I consider the Word first – before anything else concerning these matters. That is engrafted. God's Word takes priority over everything else. It becomes natural for the Christian to be more supernatural – believing and expecting God's Word to be the answer. We will become, as living epistles as Jesus The Living Word transforms us by His Word.

2 Corinthians 3: 3 You show that you are a letter from Christ, the result of our ministry, written not with ink but with the Spirit of the living God, not on tablets of stone but on tablets of human hearts.

Ephesians 6: 18 And pray in the Spirit on all occasions with all kinds of prayers and requests. With this in mind, be alert and always keep on praying for all the Lord's people.

Praying for Christians

Prayer and supplication or requests asking God for a special request for yourself or others. I want to add that we should be praying for the Christians in our lives. People such as our pastors, elders or deacons, church members we know or don't know, people who attend our church or other churches etc. We may say a brief prayer but we should care for these people. An intercessor will not only pray for his or her family but also others. Intercessors may pray for the global Church or other denominations as well as other needs. My emphasis here is to prompt you to pray for Christians. If you care about prayer – start caring about other Christians – that God would supply their needs, comfort them, strengthen them etc. This is essential if the Body of Christ is to be built up, encouraged, strengthened etc.

Families

Husbands should be praying over their wives and visa   versa.  Parents should be praying for their children. It was once the norm in the Christian Church. Parents would pray for their children, before they left for school that day. Parents would pray over their children at night. Even if the kids are grown, the parents gather them and pray for them. There is a special covering blessing when parents pray for children. There is a protection and release of God's angels to guard them. Also, the children know they are loved by the parents. A bond develops that is not there any other way. I know what it is like to not have parents that pray over you.

Once my mother became a born again- spirit filled Christian, she and I prayed together regularly. I would pray blessings over her and she for I. It was a special bond that developed between us. We had always been close, but the special prayer bond we had knit our hearts together in a special way.

Family prayer should be more than simply saying the blessing over the dinner. There should be family prayer where each member of the family is prayed for by the other members of the family. I have known Christian families that pray together in this way and they are close, loving, caring for each other. Praying with people develops a special closeness. There is a special book I want to recommend to you; it is called " The Blessing" by Smalley and Trent. It's an older book but it describes the very thing I am talking about in much detail. It discusses Biblical examples of imparting a blessing into your family by praying for them and speaking kind words over them.  I also want to mention à more current book to you on the topic by Marilyn Hickey`s `The Blessing: Generational Blessings – passing on Generational Blessings``

You may be as I was without any Christian family. Thank God I had Christian friends. As I matured as a Christian, it became important to me to be able to pray with my Christian friends. We would gather to pray together for each other. I had some friends who gathered once a month. At certain seasons, when there was a serious prayer assignment, we gathered to pray every day until a resolution to the situation occurred. True friends are friends you can pray with. People who pray together become close. A love bond develops.

Praying all Kinds of Prayer

There are all types of prayer. Some Christians only think there is one type of prayer – that is ask God for what you need. Although certainly you can ask God to supply your needs, there are other types of prayer. Don't cheapen prayer by believing it is only to ask God for something. I want to compare it to this. If you only spoke to your closest friend or your spouse to ask something of that person, that was the only communication you had with him or her, that would cheapen your relationship with that person. Our relationship is so much more. We share our heart, our hopes, our dreams, our insights; we care about the person so will speak about that person much; we care about other people that you both know etc. Relationships are not only for requests. Our relationship with God should not be less. We should care about God`s will for other people, for nations, for our community, for people we may never meet, for those who don`t know Christ.

There are different kinds of prayer. In the last chapter I mentioned those different kinds of prayer. Using the armour of God equips us for all kinds of prayer. Praying with understanding should be a normal type of prayer in our everyday lives. I literally prayer the armour of God on myself each day. It causes me to know that God is clothing me in armour of light and that He has washed me in His blood. He clothes me. It causes me and the spiritual world around me to know my righteousness is not my own but I have been given armour of light by God who shed His blood for me. Sometimes I do it more than once a day. Pray and ask the Holy spirit to quicken to you what piece of armour is required. You need to build yourself up.

During Some Seasons of Prayer

There have been certain seasons of prayer or prayer assignments as I call them, where God placed upon my spirit strongly to pray and interceded for a person or situation, it became an honour to give myself to the task. First of all, I was single, so I could focus on the prayer need. I could give myself to the task. Two of these occasions occurred while I had much time so I gave myself to hours of prayer and reading the Bible and I did not want any person of unbelief to be in my life. Please understand that I don`t believe this is the same for every person or for all seasons.

During these periods of my life, when I was totally given to prayer assignments, I was literally praying life for someone who had been declared about to die. Excluding unbelievers from your life during these serious prayer assignments is necessary. Jesus is our example in this because as he was about to raise Jairus` daughter from the dead, Jesus cleared the room of everyone but her parents and James, John, and Peter. Jesus knew who to exclude and who to include. Do you know who to exclude and who to include? It matters who is near to you when you are believing for a miracle. Doubt and unbelief have no place in your life ever if you are a Christian, and if you are believing for a miracle, you must surround yourself with people of like precious faith.

It matters who you tell your private prayer matters to. You should not share them with anyone. Just as the people I was praying for were in intensive care, surrounded by physicians and nurses and most people were excluded from their lives, so was I in the spirit, in a place of private prayer and faith. Only those of the same faith belonged there. Matters of life or death, or destiny decision making are not to be shared with just anyone. I have had glorious seasons of prayer assignments where I was knit to the people around me as closely as a hand slips into a leather glove. Those people around me were believing the same. We spoke comfort and encouragement to each other. We prayed for each other; we prayed together for miracles and saw them come to pass.

The Word of God

Hebrews 4: 12 For the word of God is alive and active. Sharper than any double-edged sword, it penetrates even to dividing soul and spirit, joints and marrow; it judges the thoughts and attitudes of the heart.

The Word of God is described as being active, quick, sharp, precise, exact. It is so powerful that it can divide soul from spirit. It is as a two-edged sword – meant for battle. It is used as a weapon that can impact tremendously. It is sharp on both sides, meaning that it is intended for mortal combat. As I have mentioned previously, a human is a spirit, has a soul and lives in a body. The Word of God is more than mere words. It has the anointing of the Holy Spirit on it to bring itself to come to pass; it can divide between soul and spirit. Only by the Holy Spirit and the discerning of spirits can a Christian know the difference between soul and spirit. The Word of God can reveal this.

Christians should be living in the Spirit and moving and having our being in the Spirit. That means we should be lead by the Holy Spirit in our lives on earth in all areas of our lives: work, school, church, society, clubs, teams, in business etc. A carnal Christian or a Christian who is living or speaking or acting from the flesh is given to all types of temptations and sins. The Word of God can reveal one's motives. It can be as a mirror that helps us to see ourselves clearly.

James 1: 23 Anyone who listens to the Word but does not do what it says is like someone who looks at his face in a mirror 24 and, after looking at himself, goes away and immediately forgets what he looks like. 25 But whoever looks intently into the perfect law that gives freedom, and continues in it—not forgetting what they have heard, but doing it—they will be blessed in what they do.

By prayerfully examining the scriptures, we can expect God to reveal areas of our lives that need light: choose them; confess them; pray them; meditate upon them. I use the word light to mean revelation – meaning spiritual transformation that comes through Divine revelation. This is an added benefit from prayerfully praying God's Word. Not only do we receive an answer to the thing or situation we are praying about, but we are also are being transformed by the Word of God from glory to glory.

Choose to be a Spirit – led Christian

A born-again spirit filled Christian should not be living in the mind, will and emotions. One who does these things is living in the realm of the soul and is as variable as the weather. They are tossed about, not having any root or foundation. Yes, they know Jesus and are saved but they are living far below their privileges as a Christian. A soulish Christian will get angry, or bitter or envious, or think too highly of himself/herself. These are things that come from the realms of the emotions. Living in the emotions is not a choice for unsaved people. They cannot help themselves, but a born-again spirit filled person can choose God's Word.

If you know there is an area that tempts you to sin – yes repent but also search the scriptures for areas that may affect you such as anger, or jealousy or pride… focus on these areas in prayer, by praying the scriptures on how to change ungodly character traits into the Biblical model – example instead of anger – patience or meekness or forbearance. As you sow the Word of God into yourself through confession and prayer, you will be transformed. You will be changed. You will develop godly character and the fruit will be evident to those around you.

If you have not heard Joyce Meyer's teachings on " I was always on my mind" I highly recommend those teachings. A person who is too self-absorbed gets into matters of the flesh. Those people actually believe all of the world revolves around them. They get offended easily; get into strife for foolish reasons etc.

Get Testimonies from People Who Have Been Transformed

Please know I realize the secular teaching that has contaminated some churches – that a person is the product of their parenting and that they have good reasons to feel that way – making excuses for living in the emotions. If any person had a right to be offended and hard hearted, it was Joyce Meyer. Listen to her testimony of how God delivered her from a terrible family situation; not only that, but God transformed her innermost being so she is peaceful and a peace maker. She gives personal testimonies of how God transformed her from a victim of life to a victor of life.

The Holy Spirit filling your spirit should be leading you. The soul should come into alignment with God's Word. You should build up your spirit by praying the Word of God, listening to worship music, worshipping, getting good preaching and teaching. Living in the spirit, you live above the situations of the earth because your center is Christ Jesus and His Word not your own desires or whims, not the ideas of people. You are in the earth, but not of the earth. You do normal stuff that other people do but you are thinking of life in matters of eternity. I give a strong word of caution about not getting into strife as it will rob you of all possible blessings God wants to bring your way.

Choosing God's Word for prayer is only effective if you believe the Bible is God's inspired Word. If you do not believe the Bible is inspired by the Holy Spirit and is without error, it is the highest standard for humans to live by on the earth, you cannot effectively use it in prayer. You should pray as you read scripture and ask God to show you and give you faith to believe and accept the Word of God.

The Bible says the Word of God is settled in heaven – it is for sure just like the sun and moon and stars are placed in the heavens – so is the Word of God certain. The Bible is our operations manual for while we are on the earth. It's a plan for us for how to live. If you have not read Dake's book 'The Plan for Man, I would recommend it. It talks about the Bible as the most important book for humans to read and gives explanations and commentary.

The Blood of Jesus

Pleading the blood is something I learned once I was born-again and in the realms of a full gospel church. I learned it early in my Christian life and I use it today more than ever before. What it means is that the person who says 'I plead the blood' is appealing to the blood of Jesus sprinkled on the mercy seat in heaven. The person is proclaiming faith in the blood of Jesus to save, heal and deliver. The person is speaking it to release faith in his or her own heart but also it is a mighty weapon against Satan and all forces of darkness. Jesus death, burial and resurrection is the way that Jesus defeated the enemy. It is because of Jesus blood that we can live in victory.

If you are facing a situation and the Holy Spirit within you prompts you to do it, plead the blood. It is usually for protection but could also be for battle when praying for Gods will in a situation. We do not come to prayer in our own righteousness. We come as blood bought people – purchased from death, hell, sin by the blood of Jesus Christ. We are made Holy by Jesus blood.

1 John 1: 7 But if we walk in the light, as he is in the light, we have fellowship with one another, and the blood of Jesus, his Son, purifies us from all[b] sin. `

Spiritual Covering

I will mention that in prayer you should have spiritual covering. First and foremost, you plead the blood of Jesus over yourself, but you should also have Christians in your life that pray for you. You should have Christians that are as a spiritual covering in your life. This may include the pastor but usually is a friend or friends who will pray for you and care for you spiritually.

Please consider this matter of having spiritual covering important. Especially it is true if you are the only Christian in your family or you are single. Spiritual covering means we are accountable to someone and someone is accountable to us. It means we remain teachable. It means we are open to correction. It should naturally occur in Christian families. It should be in Christian marriages. It should also occur in Christian friendships. We should pray protection and blessing (health, strength, prosperity) over those who are in our lives.

Jesus the Messiah fulfilled these scriptures.

Is 53: 4 Surely he took up our pain
and bore our suffering,
yet we considered him punished by God,
stricken by him, and afflicted.
5 But he was pierced for our transgressions,
he was crushed for our iniquities;
the punishment that brought us peace was on him,
and by his wounds we are healed.

Jesus took upon himself all sins, sorrows, sicknesses etc. Jesus blood is our righteousness. If God looks at you, do you know what He sees? He sees the blood of Jesus Christ covering you. God sees you as Holy because of Jesus blood. It is essential that an intercessor keep right with God and allow no place for the devil – not one sin unconfessed. If we are to minister in the place of caring for others through prayer, we have got to be clothed in Jesus blood – the armour of righteousness. If you sin, repent quickly; get up by building yourself up spiritually and don`t start sinning again. Keep going in righteousness.

The Name of Jesus

Acts 3: 16 And His name, by faith in His name, has made this man strong, whom you see and know. And faith which comes through Him has given him perfect health in your presence.

I want to emphasize these words" His name – through faith in His name" is spoken as the reason for the miracle. Do you believe in Jesus name? Jesus name is higher than all other names in heaven or earth. At the name of Jesus, every knee shall bow, every tongue confess that Jesus Christ is LORD. Faith in the name of Jesus is essential to its effectiveness in ware fare. You must believe that Jesus Christ is God who lived a holy life, suffered and died to save us, was buried and rose the third day and ascended into heaven. Faith in the name of Jesus is applying your faith in all that Jesus did and all that Jesus is. His name evokes His person. As we pray in the name of Jesus, miracles happen – not because of us but because of

Jesus. He is the eternal God who came to earth and is returning again one day.

Acts 4: 12 There is no salvation in any other, for there is no other name under heaven given among men by which we must be saved."

Jesus Christ is the highest authority there is in heaven or on earth or in places under the earth. I have met people from different countries who worship millions of gods. They have some higher and some lesser gods. They worship many. Jesus, is the only One True God – The LORD Jesus Christ. The meaning of His name is as follows: LORD meaning Jehovah (father), Jesus (spirit) Christ (anointed by the Holy Spirit). My main point is this – no false god, no demon, no person can withstand the name of Jesus. All will bow at the name of Jesus.

Romans 14: 11 For it is written:
"As I live, says the Lord,
every knee shall bow to Me,
and every tongue shall confess to God."[a]

Spiritual Warfare

As we pray, we are not simply making requests or receiving answers. In the spiritual realm there is much angelic activity as we pray. There are angels assigned by God to help bring the things we request into being. There are opposing forces or demons who are in rebellion against God and will be judged at the white throne judgement. Their fate is sealed – they will be cast into the lake of fire. They are doomed to separation from God. Until that final judgement day, they try to oppose God by fighting against us. God treasures humans above all His creation. God created humans to be in relationship with God – as intimate friends. Demons hate us because God loves us. That is why Jesus gave us these spiritual weapons so we could enforce His righteousness and bring His will to the earth until He returns.

As we pray. we must put on the armour of God; we must plead the blood; we must use the name of Jesus. We battle against spiritual beings not against people. We do not try to fight in our own strength. We must be enforcers of what Jesus has already accomplished. Jesus finished it all at Calvary. Jesus' last words "It is finished" applies to all matters of the earth past, present and future. There are other weapons such as spiritual gifts and the gift of tongues. The most powerful weapons we have cannot be understood by the wisdom of men because they are spiritual gifts. These are mighty weapons because they are enforced by Jesus Christ. They are strong because of our Faith in Jesus Christ and what He has accomplished for us.

How to Get an Answer Using the Prayer of Petition

I have talked about the armour of God and its importance but the first priority should be do you really want an answer to prayer? If you do, you will do whatever is necessary to build yourself up spiritually so you can pray in faith believing for the answer. I want to highly recommend this book "The Prayer of Petition" by Jerry Savelle. It talks about how to get answers to specific requests such as something you may want or desire or need. Example, if you need money to pay a bill or if you would like a new car. The book is very practical and expresses in much detail the method for getting an answer to a prayer request of this type.

1.   Decide what you need and write it on a piece of paper. What exactly do

you require or desire? Be specific. If it is certain amount of money, write it.

2.      Search the scriptures to find scriptures that you can pray concerning the situation. Example God promises to supply all our needs according to His riches in glory. (Phil. 4: 19)

If you want a new computer or a new car – you won't find those exact words in the Bible. But if it is a need, God promises to supply our needs. If it is a desire, God loves to give us You could use a concordance to find scriptures. I highly recommend the online reference tool Bible Gateway. Not only does it have a search engine aspect, it has multiple translations of the Bible available.

Pray the Scriptures

I also want to mention this resource if you haven't heard of it – The Christian Broadcasting Network (CBN) 700 club has a prayer altar worker's manual that includes many scriptures on various common themes people ask prayer for. It helps to categorize various prayers into categories or topics. It is an excellent reference manual. Joyce Meyer has an excellent book also, called " The Secret Power of Praying God's Word". There are some books in every Christian Bookstore about praying the promises of God, or other methods of categorizing scriptures so people can confess them and pray them. You can make up your own list but it is always wise to use resources that are excellent.

3.      Thank God for the answer before you actually see the answer with your eyes. See it with your imagination – see it as being accomplished and thank God for it. So many preachers preach on this topic but it is important to receive the answers with your faith before you receive it with your hands. Thank God for supplying it.

4.      Sow a seed of faith into a godly ministry. Literally the easiest thing to sow is money. Give a gift with expectation that you will receive an answer from God. Give into a ministry that believes the same as you or that feeds you spiritually. You could give of your time or your possessions; most people give finances because that is how we mostly do business in North America.

You could volunteer and give of yourself to a ministry or give possessions. In some countries people give a pot or a goat or something to show, they believe God will not only bless the ministry they are sowing into but also give them their heart's desire. You give of what you do have.

Don't believe in a lie that there is a magical number to give. If someone tries to charge you for praying for you or says you must give this amount for the answer – don't believe it. If God quickens a certain amount to you, you should give it. If your faith responds to a minster's call for so much money, follow the Holy Spirit's prompting.

I would give a short testimony of my own self. I was praying for myself for a job. This went on and on for years. I could get some part time but no full-time job. I heard a preacher on TV talking about this very thing. He was talking about receiving an answer to prayer and showing God you were serious by making a seed faith offering. He instructed us to wrap our faith around it and believe for God to supply. I did not have much money, but I made a vow to God. I told God I would give so much money if He would give me a job. Please know I did my part. I was sending applications; I was praying; I was updating my credentials; I was seriously seeking employment.

Within a short time, I received the job opportunity I had been praying for. It happened, and I kept my vow. I gave a very large sum of money (for me) to a ministry that I believed in, But I was so thankful to God for the job and the miraculous answer to prayer, I kept giving that amount each year. I also prayed that I could give more money to different ministries. I worked a second job so that I could give extravagantly to ministries and to people. God had released the giving gift in me through that preacher's sermon.

Praying the Scripture Means Believing it for Yourself as you Pray.

Praying the scripture is not the same as reading the scripture. Reading the scripture is good but it is not the same as praying the scripture. I am talking about literally personalizing the scripture in prayer out loud to God.

Psalm 91: 1 He who dwells in the shelter of the Most High
shall abide under the shadow of the Almighty.
2 I will say of the LORD, "He is my refuge and my fortress,
my God in whom I trust."

What I would do is pray " Thank you God that I dwell in the secret place of the most high God" Personalize it and pray it for yourself. I mean take the words and pray them over yourself or over others. If it seems awkward to you, find a translation of the Bible that is easy for you to use. Please know that reading it is not the same as praying it with faith.

# 5 THE PRAYER OF FAITH

Romans 10: 17 Consequently, faith comes from hearing the message, and the message is heard through the word about Christ.

It is saying that the Word of God has within itself the power to bring itself to come to pass by releasing faith into believers as it is spoken or preached. The hearing that is talked about is not hearing with only your natural ears but hearing with your spiritual ears. It means your heart has been softened to receive the Word of God as truth and you grab onto it mixed with faith and accept it as a personal truth from God to you. A transference occurs from you saying yes I know it is true to believing that it is true and applies directly to you.

I can explain it by explaining an example of someone who resists it. I was praying for the baptism of the Holy Spirit for someone; we were praying for a class that had been water baptized and taught the truths about the baptism of the Holy Spirit. As with anything spiritual, God will never force you to believe it; you must always have an active part of believing and receiving.

I was praying for this woman and the woman had her teeth clenched, her arms folded, her body posture completely closed as though she were trying to protect herself. She kept on saying " I don't want it. I don't want it. I don't want it." It would have been ridiculous for me to pray for her because she did not want it. If someone pits his or her human will against something – leave that person alone. God will never force Himself. Even though the Word of God was taught and preached about the truths of the Baptism of the Holy Spirit, even though people all around her were receiving the baptism of the Holy Spirit with speaking in other tongues, she did not receive the word of God with faith. She rejected it and pit herself against it.

In the same manner, as the sermon is preached or the Word of God is read aloud and you hear it with your physical ears, you have a chance to reject it by making excuses, to believe it is nice like elevator music or to receive it with faith. God's Word always brings personal decision making as it is taught or preached.

Believing it is true for you is a big part of getting something from the teaching or preaching. You speaking a word of faith out of your own mouth, speaking it quickened by faith is the best way for you to receive. You are your own best teacher. That is why we confess the promises of God to us; that is why we pray the Word of God for us. In Joshua 1 God instructs Israel to keep the Word of God before them day and night. God impresses upon Moses, later on Joshua, the importance of memorizing the scriptures and keeping them in mind. In the Old Testament, and today by Orthodox Jews, they literally attach the scripture in boxes around their foreheads and around their hands. These boxes, phylacteries, contain the scriptures – always the commandments but sometimes more. This is a symbol of what they are doing inwardly – keeping God's word as top priority.

Although I don't wear them on my arms or forehead, I do sometimes carry scriptures with me in my pocket or place it on my mirror or in the car so I will read it, pray it and study it. I have been known to receive a message from church and buy the tape or the cd and play it over and over again for weeks until the truths are deep in my heart. I also have boxes of index cards with promises of God that I am believing God for. I use them to pray, one card after the other. I don't always read all of them, but they are there to remind me of what God has promised me as a prompt in prayer and confession of God's Word.

I read the card; pray the card over and over until the engrafted word that is able to save the soul it becomes so much a part of me I believe it and it is a living part of my being. The apostle Paul says we are living epistles. The Word of God should be so much a part of us that it can come out of our mouth.

Digital media being such as it is, many young people would believe this is a primitive way of learning scripture. They could copy and paste the scripture to a page and carry it with them on their tablets or computers or phones. I like cards because slipping them in my pocket or in my car – means they are with me always. Some people are that attached to their tablets, computers or phones so it would be effective for them as well.

I have been so privileged to receive much excellent teaching and preaching in my life. There would be preaching and I would expect that the word would apply to my life. I would be sitting on the edge of my seat ready to receive the word of God preached even before the Pastor or preacher spoke it. I wanted the Word more than anything. Nothing else mattered. The Word of God spoken was what my priority was. It was like a sweet honey from a honeycomb or succulent onions and mushrooms in butter. It was ecstasy to receive that Word because I knew it applied directly to me. People who want the Word in this way are the opposite of that woman I described earlier. In. who didn't want what God promised. Instead of rejecting it – they are so eager to receive God's Word, they encourage the preacher to preach.

Desire for God's Word

These people have an attitude of God give me your word; your word is more precious than anything. Your word is life to me. Read Psalm 119. I highly recommend it as a Psalm that honours and discusses a person's love for God's Word and the priority of God's Word in your life. I have been reading through the Psalms for more than 30 years now; it is a method I learned from Bill Gauthier. Read Psalm 1 on the first; count 30 past it – read it and continue  - count 30 more and read it, until you have covered all the Psalms for that day. Also read that day's number of Proverbs. If you do this every day, you will read through all the Psalms and Proverbs in a month.

Directly reading and taking the scriptures that talk about God's love for you and God's answering prayers etc. is mostly the topic of the Psalms. I used to sigh when I got to to Psalm 119 because it is so long. In the past several years it has become my delight to read, study and pray this psalm. It has golden nuggets or aspects to it that are so profound that it makes my spirit leap. The Psalmist explains how the Word of God applies to every part of his life. Psalm 19 also discusses the love for God's Word and importance of it.

In the previous chapter, I explained how God set His name above every other name, how the name of the LORD Jesus Christ is the highest name in heaven and earth. The scripture tells us that God set His Word above His name. How magnificent is that! The Word of God is so certain it is higher than His name (Psalm 138:2). The Word of God is a living Word. It was inspired by The Holy Spirit directing holy men of God wo write it. It is quick; powerful; sharper than any two edged sword; it is the expression of the will of God for people. The word could be planted in your heart. The word grows in us as we receive it just like seed I plant in the garden grows into different kinds of plants and flowers. As we are praying the word of God for ourselves, God can bring manifold, multi-sided wisdom to us. As we are praying and meditating on the Word of God and confessing it, God can give us new revelation of how it applies to our lives and to different aspects of our lives.

Luke 11: 11 "This is the meaning of the parable: The seed is the word of God. 8 Still other seed fell on good soil. It came up and yielded a crop, a hundred times more than was sown."

The seed has the potential to bring forth a 100-fold return. Please see this – the condition of the soil, determines the productivity of the seed. All the seed is good. This is significant as we realize our hearts are the soil to receive the Word of God. If we are not willing to receive the Word, we will not receive any benefit from it; if we are willing, we can receive a 100 fold return on the word – not only in one area of our lives but in all areas of our lives; at work; at school; at church; in your clubs; on your teams; in your social life etc. God's Word can be applied to all areas of our lives and the more we pray it, meditate on it, confess it – the more God will reveal its beauty to us and the more we will be transformed by it.

Want God's Word More than Anything

Decide within yourself that you want the Word of God applied to your life, spirit, soul and body. You have got to want the Word of God in your spirit; you have got to want the word of God in your soul; you have got to want the word of God applied to your body. You've got to want it more than anything else. Should you desire it in this way, God will be directly speaking to you from His Word. God uses preachers and teachers but also, you could be reading the scriptures and it will jump at you and you know God is speaking to you.

The Word of God is the guide book for life on earth. It applies to every aspect of our human life. It was written so that God could share His heart with us about what pleases Him and what to avoid etc. It\s a book for how to live a godly life on the planet Earth. The Word produces in us fruitfulness. The book of Deuteronomy speaks of the blessings of the LORD for those who honour Him and serve Him. Read this book prayerfully. Receive it as for you personally. It explains the blessings God wants to give to His people. Deuteronomy 28 gives a list of the blessings of following God and curses should you not honour the Lord.

I mention this book of Deuteronomy because some people take vows of poverty believing that it makes them more holy. God's desire has always been to prosper us so much that we can be a blessing to those around us. He calls us trees of righteousness, the planting of the LORD (Is 61) so that we might share with those who have nothing and so that we can give to ministry and evangelism. God wants us to live in the blessing – that means the protection and provision for His people.

Deuteronomy 28:
2 All these blessings will come on you and accompany you if you obey the LORD your God:

3 You will be blessed in the city and blessed in the country.
4 The fruit of your womb will be blessed, and the crops of your land and the young of your livestock—the calves of your herds and the lambs of your flocks.
5 Your basket and your kneading trough will be blessed.
6 You will be blessed when you come in and blessed when you go out.
7 The LORD will grant that the enemies who rise up against you will be defeated before you. They will come at you from one direction but flee from you in seven.

Believe the Scripture

These scriptures show that God wants to bless you in all these areas of your life. Do you believe it? Do you receive it? You've got to believe it is God's will for you and you've got to receive it.
These are the blessings of the Old Testament. These are the blessings given to Moses. How much more has the blood of Christ made us joint heirs with Jesus? We can pray with confidence knowing His blood made the way for us to enter the Holiest place. These scriptures are for us to take personally. They apply to us. We have been engrafted into the side of Jesus Christ – now made an heir with Jesus of all the promises of God to Abraham, Isaac, Jacob, Moses etc.

Pray the Scripture

Literally praying these scriptures over yourself in faith believing that God will give you these things He has promised is essential. You must believe that He has given them to us and that He wants us to have them. It is not only financial though. The blessings of God are for every area of your life. Praying the kind of prayers that the apostle Paul prayed will get you results in other areas of your life also.

Ephesians 1: 15 For this reason, ever since I heard about your faith in the Lord Jesus and your love for all God's people, 16 I have not stopped giving thanks for you, remembering you in my prayers. 17 I keep asking that the God of our Lord Jesus Christ, the glorious Father, may give you the Spirit[f] of wisdom and revelation, so that you may know him better. 18 I pray that the eyes of your heart may be enlightened in order that you may know the hope to which he has called you, the riches of his glorious inheritance in his holy people, 19 and his incomparably great power for us who believe.

This is a type of thanksgiving prayer thanking God for the people and an intercessory prayer praying for spiritual revelation. This is praying for God to reveal His glory to you. This is a prayer to pray over yourself. Pray that God would help you to understand more of the Word of God. Pray that you might know Him more. Ask God for wisdom, knowledge and revelation.

Expect for Him to impart it to you. The Holy Spirit will release new measures of the glory of God to you. Ask and believe that God will give you wisdom. There are depths in the riches of the glory of Christ. If you earnestly desire more of God, He will continuously transform you from glory to glory.

Pray for Wisdom

I pray for wisdom for all parts of my life. I want words of wisdom for me at school. I want words of wisdom in the community. I want words of wisdom in my church. I want them at home. Don't only believe it is for one thing alone. God's Word can apply to all areas of your life. There can be a 100-fold increase of God's Word applied to all areas of your life as you apply God's scriptures with revelation. This comes through praying the scriptures and taking them personally.

God gives us blessings for all areas of our lives physical, financial, for your soul, for your relationships etc. As we begin to pray to apply God's word to our lives, God will increase our capacity to receive from Him in those areas.

Increase your Capacity to Receive

I want to express it to you such as this; a cup can hold a cup of water. My tap turned on flows more than a cupful. I could use a pot and it would hold more water. I could use a bathtub; it would be more. The truth is I could fill a swimming pool with water from a tap. With God, there is no limit to what He can or will do for us. It depends on our capacity to receive. We should literally pray for God to increase our capacity to receive. This will mean God will grow us in such a way that we can learn more about him and can receive more from Him.

Jesus our Intercessor

As you are praying, Jesus is the author of your faith (Hebrews 12: 2). Jesus is the high priest (Hebrews 4: 14-16) over your profession of faith. Jesus is not only passively hearing your prayers. He is giving you faith as you read the word, pray the word and confess the word. Jesus is also your prayer partner. His blood gave Him the authority to be your LORD. It made a way for you to enter The Throne room of God. Jesus is interceding for you. Your responsibility to read the word, confess the Word and pray the Word.

There was a time in my life where I made faith tapes for myself. I taped scriptures I was believing God for and played them over and over so the Word would get on the inside of me. Even people in a coma can receive the word of God. The spirit is quickened by the Word of God. I have prayed over people in a coma, and spoken prayers of faith over them, knowing they could not hear me with their physical ears but their spirits could receive. There are so many ministries that have scriptures on CD's or tapes for you to play to get the Word of God on the inside of you but let me share with you; your own voice speaking the Word of God with faith is the strongest influence on your own life. I would recommend you make a tape or CD of God's special scriptures for you and play it over and over, your own voice speaking life.

Some people find it hard to memorize scripture, so a technique to help you would be to turn it into song. Sing it. If you don't know how to create a melody, take a melody you already know and sing the scripture to it.

Get the Word on the Inside of you

As a new Christian, I would read the Bible in spurts on my own. Soon, a teacher introduced me to the read through the Bible in a year Bible and it made me more of a consistent reader of the Word. As I grew in Christ, I began to want to read through the Bible more than once a year. I wanted to study it in chunks. I became quite passionate about the Word the more I studied it, and even in my secular job, I would bring a Bible and at lunch, I would lock my door and read the Bible. I wanted the Word more than I

wanted the gossip at work. I wanted the Word more than I wanted anything else.

I would dig into parts of scripture and I found God was quickening the scriptures to me more throughout my day. I would be talking with someone at my job and I would speak the scripture to people in words of wisdom, or words of encouragement. What this does, getting the scripture on the inside of you as I call it is build your faith to receive from God so that when you pray, you can pray with wisdom (knowing what God's Word states) and faith believing the Word and knowing the God who can bring it to pass.

I encourage you to make a spiritual investment in your own spiritual life. You must get the Word of God into you yourself. Buy yourself CDs, DVDs, music etc. that will help to build up your spirit. Read the Bible prayerfully.

Build up your faith by praying scripture over your situations or people. As you pray the Word of God over yourself and others, you release faith in the scripture; more faith is released as you hear yourself praying the prayer of faith. It not only is praying God's will for somebody, but it is building you up in the faith.

The Prayer of Faith – can be prayed with confidence knowing it is God's will because it is in the Word.

Often only Needed one Prayer

There are situations where you may pray the prayer of faith over a situation and it will immediately be answered. I mean it may manifest in the natural realm almost immediately. There are other times that you pray the prayer of faith and you know that you have received the answer by faith. Start praising God and thanking Him for the answer. If you know that you have the answer (by the spirit) start thanking God and keep thanking Him and praising Him until you see the answer manifest in the natural.

Usually the Gift of Faith is used with this Prayer

In special situations such as a life or death situation, or destiny decision, God grants us the gift of faith. This is more than ordinary faith that is released by hearing the Word of God. The gift of faith is supernatural faith through the Holy Spirit to believe for miracles.

James 5: 13-15

13 Is anyone among you in trouble? Let them pray. Is anyone happy? Let them sing songs of praise. 14 Is anyone among you sick? Let them call the elders of the church to pray over them and anoint them with oil in the name of the Lord. 15 And the prayer offered in faith will make the sick person well; the Lord will raise them up. If they have sinned, they will be forgiven.

The scripture instructs us on how to minister to the sick. The elders or mature Christians should pray over them anointing them with oil which is a symbol of the Holy Spirit. They are to pray for healing. They are not to wonder if the person will live or die. The prayer of faith prays God's Word. Jesus healed the sick. Jesus heals the sick today through those who believe and pray the prayer of faith. I have received this ministry on several occasions in my life. I have also ministered to others this sacrament. You place the oil on the person imparting the life of Christ. The Holy Spirit using you to be a point of contact laying hands on someone is miraculous. God can impart to you faith for a miracle and through you the healing power of Christ.

Warning:

If someone tries to lay hands on you in unbelief – run from them. Do not just let anyone lay hands on you. They should be people known to you as elders in the church or ministers of the LORD. If the person prays in unbelief at all as to whether God wants to heal you or not, get away from that person so he or she cannot touch you. Don't receive a prayer of unbelief over you when you are believing for a miracle. If they are not sure the LORD wants to heal you, those people have got nothing in common with you.

The scripture states the prayer of faith shall save the sick. The prayer of faith – we believe – we literally impart faith for a miracle and the healing power of God. One funny instance I recall is a testimony of a man and his wife who were praying over their baby. They didn't know what to do exactly but they read it in the Bible and believed it so they put their baby in a bathtub and poured a bottle of oil over the kid. The kid was slippery because they put so much oil. God answered their prayer and healed the baby because He saw their faith.

I saw my own mother near death, in a coma, hooked up to machines for breathing, etc. Doctors let me know there was a chance she may not live. I sat there praying and praying. I was praying for a miracle. I believed God would do a miracle. I begged the nurses to let me stay there and pray late into the evenings. I went on my lunch hour. I prayed over her scripture, believing God was there with me – with her. I called everyone I knew that could pray to pray. I sent out prayer requests to ministries. The elders came and prayed for my mum and anointed her with oil. I got a prayer cloth and had it anointed with oil with faith and I pinned it to her hospital gown. Within three days, she was sitting up in her hospital bed taking communion with me. She was off all those machines except for the heart monitor.

Thank God I have seen the prayer of faith in action. I told of my Pastor who was on his death bed; the doctors said he probably wouldn't live. They were so negative, any time we heard from them we immediately were pleading the blood over him and his relatives. We started praying scriptures. In a life or death situation, you cannot be moved by what you hear or what you see. You must believe the Word of God and pray in faith until the natural aligns with God's Word.

Remember secular doctors are confined to the 3 dimensions of this earth. We are not confined – we can have confidence to enter the most Holy place praying to Jesus who paid the price for all sin, sickness, disease etc. by dying on the cross. Jesus is the resurrection and the life.

Pray in Faith for those who Cannot Pray for Themselves

The scripture says " If they have sinned, they will be forgiven." The prayer of faith ministers to the spirit, the soul and the body of the person. Jesus ministers to the whole person. We have by faith the anointing to minister healing to all parts of a person. This does not replace repentance by the person, but if the person cannot pray for himself or herself, we can minster in faith.

If someone has sinned against you, you have the authority to forgive that person for what he or she has done. You can plead the blood over those people forgiving them and praying for mercy on them. Truly they require mercy because if they have sinned against you, God will judge them.

Mark 2: 2 They gathered in such large numbers that there was no room left, not even outside the door, and he preached the word to them. 3 Some men came, bringing to him a paralyzed man, carried by four of them. 4 Since they could not get him to Jesus because of the crowd, they made an opening in the roof above Jesus by digging through it and then lowered the mat the man was lying on. 5 When Jesus saw their faith, he said to the paralyzed man, "Son, your sins are forgiven."

This scripture talks about Jesus and that there were so many people gathered. There was no room for any more people. I have been to meetings like this my own self where there are thousands of people gathered to worship, praise and hear the Word of God. The largest meeting, I believe, I have been in is about 20, 000 people in a service. I know there are larger gathering but I haven't been in them yet. There are places in Africa they gather a million people or more; they use technology to broadcast and to project the preaching to all those people.

Those guys wanted to bring their paralyzed friend on that stretcher to Jesus. They knew if they could get that man to Jesus, he could be healed. It wasn't even the man on the stretcher that has the faith in this situation. It was the faith of those man's friends. They climbed up on the roof and made a whole in the roof and lowered their friend down to Jesus' feet. Those men took bold faith to do what they did. They believed Jesus could and would heal their friend.

Jesus Sees Your Faith

Jesus saw the men's faith and spoke a word of forgiveness of sins and also healing. In this case (not all only this one in particular) the disease was connected to some sin. Jesus forgave the sins and healed the man. The people there were outraged at Jesus forgiving sins. The man was healed and got up at the Word of the LORD.

# 6 PRAYER OF DEDICATION AND CONSECRATION

The prayer of Consecration and dedication has got to be one of the most misunderstood types of prayer there is. There is a proper use for it but some people believe it is the only type of prayer, so they apply this to all situation, using it incorrectly. It is important to consecrate ourselves to God – that means to wholly give yourself – spirit, soul and body to God. It is not a one-time prayer as some people believe that it is. When you first accept Jesus Christ as your Saviour, you pray this type of prayer accepting Him to be your Saviour and your LORD. You give yourself to God. But that is not the only time you should pray consecrating yourself to the LORD.

Dedicate yourself is to give yourself wholly; consecrate means to be separated unto God. Giving yourself to God can include submission of your human will. An example of the prayer of consecration and dedication is when Jesus prays in the Garden of Gethsemane and prays not my will but yours be done. (Mark 14: 36) He submits his human will to God's plan of salvation that will be a result of his death, burial and resurrection. There are certainly opportunities to pray this type of prayer.

I have known of preachers who know they could be in a comfortable place in North America preaching and teaching but they feel the call of God to go preach in countries with scorching heat and humidity and less than best living conditions. I have known of people who accept tough assignments from God. An example is my friend who was living quite comfortable in Canada and finally got her house paid for, but felt the prompting of the LORD to give the house (the value of the home) to the Church for the building of a Christian Church. There were others in the congregation who did the same thing. They knew God's will was the build the local church so they gave all they owned.

This type of prayer means you give all you can for the will of God, often with personal sacrifice. People take this prayer totally out of context and misuse it when they use it instead of some of the other types of prayer.

Example, if you need a job, you should be asking in faith, believing God will answer your petition. You should not be praying "If it be your will". It is always the will of God to prosper you. Someone who prays "if it be your will" for salvation or healing, or petitions or intercession is praying amiss. They are not lining up with scripture.

Let's start with "If it be your will, heal me." This is misuse of this prayer. In Isaiah 53, we learn that the Messiah (Jesus) suffered and died so that we might be saved, healed, delivered etc. God would not clearly state His will for us in scripture and contradict Himself by not willing for our healing. God's Word is a statement of His will. I have discussed the value of God's Word in practically every chapter but to be able to pray effectively, one must know what God's Word states. You must line up your faith with God's Word. Our faith is not mysterious or weird – we literally believe the Bible is God's Word – His will for us spoken to Holy men of God who wrote as the Holy Spirit gave them utterance.

This prayer of submitting your will to God's will is only applicable in these types of situations:
1.	Giving yourself to God for salvation
2.	Re-dedicating your life to Christ
3.	Choosing God's way rather than a way of the flesh (sin)
4.	Choosing God's way (He will speak to you) rather than a way more comfortable
5.	If you do not know what God is asking of you but you know He is requiring more of you. Never use the prayer of consecration and dedication in these situations:
6.	When you are praying for petitions or making requests of God for daily needs or things. God says to ask and believe that He will supply.
7.	Instead of the prayer of Faith when you are praying for healing or miracles. The prayer of faith will heal the sick. A prayer of if it be thy will was corrected by Jesus in Luke 5: 12. The leper said to Jesus, if it be your will heal me.,, Jesus answered and said I will and touched him and he was healed.
8.	Instead of a prayer of repentance to receive Jesus' forgiveness. It is always God's will to forgive you.

1 Thessalonians 5:23 Is the Apostle Paul states the following prayer: 23 May God himself, the God of peace, sanctify you through and through. May your whole spirit, soul and body be kept blameless at the coming of our Lord Jesus

Christ. 24 The one who calls you is faithful, and he will do it.

He is praying for the people to be wholly consecrated to God. I would like to explain what that means. It means that Jesus living on the inside of you is always the priority. It means God is communing with you throughout the day. It means your words, thoughts and deeds line up with God or you immediately repent and consecrate yourself fresh. A person wholly consecrated will always pray about major decisions; he or she will invite God into the midst of his or her workplace; he or she will live the same at home and in public as he or she lives in church. The person is completely, genuinely God's servant.

Fresh Consecration

There are special times the Spirit of the LORD will move on a congregation for fresh consecration. It may be the preacher who brings a message with an altar call that follows. It may be during praise and worship that the Holy Spirit compels people to come forward to the altar to recommit their lives to God. If it happens at your church, you will never forget it. Your heart will feel a longing for more of God; there will be opportunity to go forward to make a physical move of your body from your usual place to a place of making an altar – or kneeling or standing as though before God's throne. You present yourself wholly.

There is no shame in fresh commitment; whether it is repenting of sin or a fresh renewal of your vow to live for God or a new level of dedication, you should never be ashamed of giving yourself to God. Jesus wasn't ashamed to die on the cross for us; he did it bruised and bleeding and in sorrow and pain, yet He accepted it knowing it meant that you and I could be free; He knew His blood shed for us was the only way to make peace with God.

The Apostle Paul said " 1 Corinthians 15:31 I face death every day— yes, just as surely as I boast about you in Christ Jesus our Lord. (NIV)
The King James says " I die daily". What this means is risking your life to preach when people would reject you and stone you or you could be arrested because it wasn't legal.

There are pastors and Christians who do this daily in our earth. There are countries where there is no freedom of worship. Christians face jail or death for proclaiming their faith or sharing Christ with others. It also means dying to doing whatever else you want to preach or teach Christ as the priority. It may mean doing something radical like becoming a missionary or it could mean giving yourself more to God in prayer and fasting.

Christ living in us can empower us to give ourselves wholly to preach or teach or worship or pray or do something for God that no one else you know may be doing. Just because the people you know are not living radically for Christ, doesn't mean there are not Christians living radically. It is easier to fast and pray when the whole church is fasting and praying than if God tugs at your heart and leads you to fast and pray.

Psalm 40:
7 Then I said, "Here I am, I have come—
it is written about me in the scroll.[e]
8 I desire to do your will, my God;
your law is within my heart." (NIV)

The scripture above is one of my favorite scriptures. My pastor was teaching and during the teaching, this was just one of the scriptures he used and it jumped out at me. I grabbed on it and started praying it for myself. It literally means that you present yourself to God saying the Word of God is my delight – I live by the Word of God; these words apply to my life directly. I identify with the Word of God for my life personally. Your Word, your will, your way. I conform to your Word.

Romans 12: 1 Therefore, I urge you, brothers and sisters, in view of God's mercy, to offer your bodies as a living sacrifice, holy and pleasing to God—this is your true and proper worship. 2 Do not conform to the pattern of this world, but be transformed by the renewing of your mind. Then you will be able to test and approve what God's will is—his good, pleasing and perfect will. (NIV)

God is Holy – Be a living Holy sacrifice. Give your life to God. In the Old Testament, they offered animals as sacrifice. The most pleasing thing we can give to God is our lives. We should do this daily. Each day invite the Holy Spirit to lead you and guide you throughout the day. Throughout the day be in communion with God to see if He would want you to pray for someone or give something to someone. He may ask you to help someone. Freely offer yourself that God may use your life to help others and bring Him much glory.

Be not conformed to this world. There is the society we live in and the whole earth we live in that has its own ways. These include trends in fashion, entertainment and business. It includes politics and religion. It includes the way we think about family. It is mostly decided by the people of their nations and its laws but also is taught in school and projected by the media as the norm. Christians are not to conform to these ways in any ways that contradict the Word of God. We are to keep God's Word first. In North America, there is a strong drive to consumerism. Buy the best...Buy new... Buy one better than your neighbor... Try to get above by buying the best... You deserve the best... Indulge...

These are just some of the slogans that are used and pictures and video and music is created to promote these beliefs.

Consumerism: The Best of What Money Can Buy

I thank God for the freedoms we have in North America. We do have freedom to choose our own live styles. We can choose to live radically for Jesus. I thank God for the arts and the entertainment and the media; our countries are informed. It is easy to find out what is going on anywhere in the earth because of our excellence in these aspects of society. But I do not worship these aspects of society. They are trying to sell to us – to spend money – to buy the best etc. but you can decide what is necessary and what isn't. We cannot let money be a god to us. We should not let things be more important than God or people.

We are to be transformed by the renewing of our minds – by the WORD of God. God's Word emphasizes God's will and what is best for us. The two are the same. God's will is always the best for us.

If you do not know the will of God concerning a situation, pray and search the scriptures prayerfully for scriptures pertaining to your situation. I have met many young people and older people who don't know what they are to do or which way to go. Teenagers want to do one thing; their parents might want something else for them. They don't know which way to go in terms of education or training or life goals etc. If you do not know which way to go and you do not have a scripture, consecrate yourself to God fresh. You may want to fast and pray. Fasting causes us to willingly give up food or drink to seek God more fervently. Use that time to pray more. Seek the LORD for an answer to your situation.

Find scriptures to pray such as James 1: 5 If any of you lacks wisdom, you should ask God, who gives generously to all without finding fault, and it will be given to you. 6 But when you ask, you must believe and not doubt, because the one who doubts is like a wave of the sea, blown and tossed by the wind.

Separate yourself from your usual activities and spend that time seeking God. Expect that God will direct you. Consecrate yourself to His will and pray that He lead you in decision making. God will either speak to you a Word that will show you the direction or He will let you feel His peace in decision making. Do what you know to do;, do it with all your heart; you know it is right to pray; you know it is right to read your Bible; you know its right to pray scripture. Worship and thank God for making a way to communicate with you. Do the right thing over and over and over; Keep believing that God will speak to you. He will.
Let Peace Be Your Umpire

I got it from Gloria Copeland. That is to pray by saying aloud " Lord let peace be my umpire. I believe this is what I am going to do;[ say it out loud speaking to God]  if it is not what you want me to do, please correct me," The Holy Spirit will give you peace or a check in your spirit.

One example of this was very early on in my Christian life, maybe a week or so saved. I didn't know if God wanted me to continue in school or not. You see, salvation was explained to me as a very serious decision that meant giving all your life to God. I was willing to do anything God asked of me. I prayed and I didn't even know much about reading the Bible; I would turn to it and read the scripture but not even in an orderly fashion or anything. God was so merciful to me. I turned to a scripture and it jumped off the page at me. I knew God was speaking to me directly.

1 Corinthians 7: 20 Each person should remain in the situation they were in when God called them.

I knew the Word of God was for me directly as it was exactly the matter I had been praying about. Tremendous peace came to me as I read that Word. I knew I should continue my studies at school. Now I don't suggest your randomly choose words from the Bible. But please know I didn't even know that scripture existed. I had not studied the Bible before. I didn't know what God's Word said. He was so merciful to me that He lead me. I got some excellent teaching in the Bible in my Christian life. God cares for all levels of Christians, whether they be seasoned saints or new born Christians who don't know God's Word.

Well, I completed all my studies and graduated and I applied to Teacher's College. It was a new direction but not new to me. I had wanted to be a teacher since I was a child. At the age of 4 or 5, I was teaching my teddy bears and dolls. As soon as I got to grade one and started being able to read words, I started teaching kids younger than me. We would play school and I would make them read, spell and do math. I wanted to be a teacher. I wanted it all my life. But after I became a Christin, I never talked about it with God. I had that one confirmation word to keep doing what you are doing. I didn't understand that God wanted to be a part of all parts of my life.

I had good grades but not an A average. It was an A-. I got a letter from the teacher's college that said I was not accepted. I couldn't believe it. It caused me to be very perplexed as I wanted it more than anything else. I prayed about it. I believed the LORD spoke to me that I never asked Him about it. I didn't even know He cared about it. I repented and said, God I want to do this with all my heart, but if you have something else for me, I'll do it.

God said I didn't say I didn't want you to be a teacher; I said I wanted you to talk about it with me. This is how I started learning that God cares about all my life choices and will give me direction and leading. What I learned was that God wanted to be included in all major decisions of my life. I should have prayed about it. If there is any change of direction, we should consult God. At that point, I believed God would make a way for me to be accepted or I would get further educational opportunities or a job or other opportunities.

Within a short time, maybe one or two weeks or so, I received a second letter telling me I was accepted into Teacher's College. Those weeks I kept trusting God to provide direction to me. God let me know it wasn't that He didn't want me to be a teacher; what He wanted is for me to talk to Him about it. God wants us to share all aspects of our lives with Him.

Philippians 2: 13 for it is God who works in you to will and to act in order to fulfill his good purpose. 14 Do everything without grumbling or arguing,

Dying to Your Old Nature

As a new Christian, I remember learning about right from wrong from the point of view of Scripture. Some of what I loved doing, sinning, was directly against the Word of God. I used to pray God help me to love what you love and hate what you hate. I believed God who revealed His will to me would also cause me to be conformed to the Word – transformed by the Word and the Spirit. Once you become a Christian, you won't want to sin. You will be praying for God to help you to live Holy. You dedicate all your life to Him. God will by His Spirit moving within you transform you. God will give you Christian friends. True Christian friends will do whatever they can to help you live in the high call of God for your life – a life without sin. Pray for God to give you those types of friends.

I pray for those of you who are rededicating your lives to God. May God separate you unto Himself for His glory. May God strengthen you and cause you to grow in desire for the Word of God and prayer.

I pray for those who are giving their lives to God for a career. May God use you to learn all you can so that you might be a light for Christ in your schools and in your professions. I pray for Christian teachers, plumbers, truck drivers, doctors, dentists, carpenters, executives. May God release you to use your gifts and talents to glorify Him as you give yourself completely to God.

# 7 CASTING YOUR CARES

This prayer of casting your cares onto the LORD is important as there are situations in life that are out of our control. Unresolved issue such as separation or divorce, friends that are distant, injustice that is not explained, things out of our control – it is important to trust the one who can do all things. Literally, in this prayer, you are professing faith in the Lord's Omnipotence and trusting His wisdom in answering the situation in the best possible way. It involves faith and consistency on your part.

Casting means to throw – it literally involves throwing your cares away – onto the LORD – that He might resolve it in the best way possible beyond human understanding. This is the exact opposite of what the word would teach. The word – Eon- this present age we live in is often affected by changes in the economy, war, poverty, etc. We as Christians also have such situations – but the difference is hope and faith in Christ. The secular media broadcasts negative news. People report things as they see them: the economy is poor; the jobless rate is higher; there were murders; there is injustice. It sends a negative message.

Faith is the Opposite of The World's Way

The world's ways of handling these types of things is to discuss them – usually in a negative complaining way as though there is no solution. The lie is that talking about negative things makes you feel better. It doesn't; what it does is cause you to doubt the security of your life and of others. It leaves unhappy and fearful.

Although it is excellent to get accurate information from media sources, the truth is beyond those events. As Christians, we live believing in hope of Christ's return. We also have been given authority over the spheres of authority of our lives. We can make a difference. By praying, by serving, by giving, we can affect the community we live in. When it seems impossible, beyond what we can do – we must trust the One who can change all things by leaving our care with Him.

This sounds so simple, but to many people it is not that easy. People who are new Christians or new to a life of faith, don't know how to cast it.

What happens is they may pray " Lord I give you the care of this matter" but as soon as it comes to mind again, they begin to worry and wonder and imagine and get themselves into a place of fear so that they have lost their peace.

If the care turns into fear and comes to your mind, speak the word out loud so your own ears can hear you: "I gave that care to the LORD and I am believing that He will take care of it because He cares for me. " You may say I did that but it came back. So you say it and say it and say it until it doesn't come back anymore. You must keep fear, unbelief, worry, wasted energy on matters beyond your control completely out of your life. Give it to God who can give you the best.

The way of the Kingdom of God is this way: if there is any ruffle in your peace – anything that is giving you fear or apprehension or worry – give it to God. Of course, you should do everything you can do in the natural. If there is a difference you can make, you should do it. Do whatever you can do and trust the rest of it to God. Believe that He will care for you because the scriptures tell us He does.

The Cares of the World

I am in no way belittling the situations that could come in your life and cause you concern. We live in a world that needs a Saviour. There are signs of the curse upon Adam on earth: death, disease, poverty, injustice, lack, suffering etc. It is not that these things are not important. They are vitally important and as Christians we should care for these things. We should pray. We should do what we can do; if we can give, if we can serve, we should. Beyond that – we must commit it to God. This is the best possible person to commit these matters too. He cares for those people more than we do; He can cause others to rally and solve things; He can provide miraculous solutions to those situations.

What I am saying is that after you've done all you can, cast your care on the LORD believing the truth: He cares for you. His Word can bring itself to come to pass. He can give you perfect peace no matter what your situation is. Your confidence is not in the situation or luck or chance. The world system loves to estimate chance and percentages etc. For instance, they may give a person a 20% chance of recovery. Our confidence must be in the God who can do all things. If you do not know that God can and will take your cares from you – your god is too small. You do not know the Almighty God of Israel.

Build up your Faith

God's Word has within itself the power to bring itself to come to pass. As we pray the Word of God mixed with faith, an explosion occurs in the Spirit realm and God manifest miracles. I'm not just talking about one miracle; I am saying there could be a series of miracles. First of all it is a miracle that you can have peace in a storm. Also, the God who can speak peace to the storm and cause relief to come is caring for the matter for you.

Let me give you an example in an ordinary situation. As a child I played every sport possible. If I had a piece of sports' equipment that was faulty, I fixed it myself. If it was beyond me – I couldn't fix it, I'd give it to my dad. He could always repair anything. Once I gave the equipment to my dad, I no longer worried about it. I knew he could repair it or show me what to do. I trusted knowing he was the expert. It is the same type of trust we must have with God; we commit our care of the situation onto the person who can and will solve it.

First you must recognize if this is a situation that requires this type of prayer solution. Pray for wisdom and discernment that you might know your situation. Christians who know what it is like to live in peace will immediately recognize the situation. Once you give your life to Christ, you know what it is like to have the Holy spirit, the Spirit of peace come live inside of you. God is with us 24/7 -365 – Wherever you go, God goes with you; Never again are you alone. In His presence is peace. If you know the peace of God, you most certainly realize it if the peace of God is missing. If you are not feeling peace – you know it is not God. It is an indicator that we must pray about the situation.

I know personally what it is like to be in a situation totally beyond my control. There was nothing I could do but be the best I could be in an unpleasant situation. I was overwhelmed. But God spoke from within my spirit so I spoke it over my own self this scripture:

1 Timothy 1: 7 For God has not given us the spirit of fear, but of power, and love, and self-control.

Oh! That Word gave me boldness. That word caused me to be strengthened and I spoke it to myself daily. I prayed it. I confessed it out loud so I could hear my own mouth speaking. God was letting me know, He was with me and He would care for me. He would take from me my cares about the situation and in a right way care for me to see it through. I committed myself to Him that day. Throughout the years, that same Word was the answer repeatedly. Fear does not come from God. If you are fearful, it means you are not living in perfect love.

1 John 4: 18 There is no fear in love, but perfect love casts out fear, because fear has to do with punishment. Whoever fears is not perfect in love.

A Christian should not be living in fear. It is not that there are not dangers or trials; it is that our God lives in us and He gives us peace – no matter what. It's an awesome way to be a testimony to the people around us. It is not a normal worldly reaction – peace in a storm. But God can and does give it.

Fear is from the devil. It can paralyze you; it can stop you from functioning normally. Faith is an injection of boldness that comes when we pray the Word of God and speak the Word of God over our selves. We build up ourselves in the Holy Faith as the scriptures commands us.

Ephesians 5: 19 Speak to one another in psalms, hymns, and spiritual songs, singing and making melody in your heart to the Lord. 20 Give thanks always for all things to God the Father in the name of our Lord Jesus Christ, 21 being submissive to one another in the fear of God.

Jude 1: 20 But you, beloved, build yourselves up in your most holy faith. Pray in the Holy Spirit.

God brings peace. Jesus is the prince of peace. It's not a saying only; it is truth. As a dark room is lit if you bring a light into it, Jesus brings His peace into your life as you draw near to him.

1 Peter 5: 6 Humble yourselves under the mighty hand of God, that He may exalt you in due time. 7 Cast all your care upon Him, because He cares for you.

A proud person will not easily come to Christ. If a person believes he or she doesn't need God, that person will not be submitted to God or His Word. It requires humility to trust God with something beyond us. It acknowledges we need Him. Pride is a sin. It caused Lucifer to lose his place and be cast out of heaven as Satan. A proud person will not want to submit to God.

Humility in Casting Your Care

Casting all your care is the opposite of pride. It is confessing and believing that if we give it to Jesus Christ, He will take care of it and we can have peace knowing this. We give it to the best person to care for it. We entrust it to the highest authority. God is not limited by the scientific dynamics of the planet Earth or our universe. He can see things past, present and future at a glance. God knows what to do and as we commit our cares to Him, He releases His peace in our lives.

There are times that as we are praying, God lets us see things from the heavenly realm. These special glimpses help to build our faith and show us there is so much more going on than what we humans can conceive of. God sees things from on the Throne in glory. Jesus triumphed over death, hell and the grave. Jesus is awaiting the moment when the Spirit and Bride on the earth cry Come Lord Jesus and Jehovah says "Go" The day of His return to earth will reveal Him in glory as ruler on Earth as He sets up His throne in Jerusalem.

At one point in my life in training for ministry and volunteering in the Church in in a Christian Missionary organization, I had a situation arise. My mother became deathly ill. I prayed; I got everybody I knew to pray. I had commitments at Church and at the Missionary organization, plus my job. I was overwhelmed. As I prayed I felt very strongly that God was letting me know that if I kept doing my best for Him, He would care for the matters I couldn't. I literally felt His peace that He would care for my mum. He was faithful; He extended her life by several years.

I have heard of so many testimonies of parents about their kids. For instance, their kids were not following the LORD as they could, or their kids were staying out late at night and they didn't know with whom or why or what they were doing. These parents had God reveal to them to trust God with their kids – literally praying protection and blessing over the kids and expecting that God would care for them. Some of these testimonies include the young adult confessing that at a certain time he or she felt an impression not to go to a place even though they wanted to, and by the person obeying that prompting, the person was spared grief or tragedy.

Keep out of Fear

Any type of fear, anxiety, feeling overwhelmed by the cares of life does not come from God. These things will waste our life energy. These things will rob us of our peace but more than that, they may cause us to be in unbelief which is sin and the results of sin are always death. I do not have to be a partaker in the world's fears or worries. I heard Kenneth Copeland give a strong message stating I do not have to be a part of the economic recessions. He preached to all his partners that none of us had to be partakers of the Babylonian system of the earth. We could live by faith and see God's miraculous supply. Our focus doesn't have to be limited to our senses. We can live above the earth while we are on the earth. We live by a higher standard. Living by faith involves seeing the miraculous in our lives regularly.

Ways to protect yourself from falling into the fear of the world or the cares of this world are to pay attention to what we are watching (TV, Movies etc.), what we are listening to (music – lyrics matter), what we are spending our efforts focusing on. Giving ourselves to the world's perspective of life will cause fear. The media is saturated with fear and doom. It is your responsibility to keep yourself from these influences and to protect your children while they are under your supervision. Instead of watching and absorbing the negative garbage, you could be speaking faith, living by faith, talking faith etc. and see the miraculous provision of God in any situation. Choose carefully who you associate with. Choose people of faith, that you might see the blessing of the Lord on you; these people will encourage you and bring out the best in you; they will inspire you to be what God created you to be.

In a recession, while other people are worrying and fretting, God can be giving you inventions and solutions. God can cause you to be a part of the solution. Remember how God used Joseph a slave in prison, to find a solution for all of Egypt. God raised him up out of the prison and gave him authority. O that God would raise up some Christians into positions of authority who would influence their nations because God will be guiding them and directing them through the situations of life.

Romans 14: 17 For the kingdom of God does not mean eating and drinking, but righteousness and peace and joy in the Holy Spirit.

Philippians 4: 6 Be anxious for nothing, but in everything, by prayer and supplication with gratitude, make your requests known to God. 7 And the peace of God, which surpasses all understanding, will protect your hearts and minds through Christ Jesus. 8 Finally, brothers, whatever things are true, whatever things are honest, whatever things are just, whatever things are pure, whatever things are lovely, whatever things are of good report, if there is any virtue, and if there is any praise, think on these things.

Isaiah 53: 5B the chastisement of our peace was upon him,
and by his stripes we are healed.

Jesus death and resurrection brought our salvation, Healing,

Deliverance and He took upon Himself any cares or worries. He gives us peace. His peace is eternal, but we must claim it for our own selves. It is not enough to simply know it. We must appropriate it by claiming His privileges. Read the Word; confess the Word; pray the Word; sow the Word into yourself and others. Truly it is the answer of how to know the peace of God.

May the peace that passes all understanding keep your heart and mind. It says peace that passes understanding, This truth has at least two applications. One is to know peace that goes beyond all normal peace. You can be calm even though you are in a storm. Secondly, peace that passes understanding is also peace that can bring you understanding and wisdom of God concerning your life and the situations of your concern. He can give a peace that cannot be explained because God can lift you above your circumstance to see it in light of eternity.

Ephesians 1: 20 which He performed in Christ when He raised Him from the dead and seated Him at His own right hand in the heavenly places, 21 far above all principalities, and power, and might, and dominion, and every name that is named, not only in this age but also in that which is to come.

Jesus is seated at the right hand of Jehovah in heaven. All things are subject to His authority. His victory over death and redemption of mankind is eternal. The Scripture tells us He is interceding and praying for us. The fact that we can boldly enter into communion through prayer to the Most High God is pretty amazing, but it is even more awesome than that. Although we enter God's presence through praise and worship and prayer, He lifts us up to be with Him in communion with Him as we pray. We become One with the Almighty – seated with Him in heavenly places.

God Can Raise us Above the Situation

Ephesians 2: But God, being rich in mercy, because of His great love with which He loved us, 5 even when we were dead in sins, made us alive together with Christ (by grace you have been saved), 6 and He raised us up and seated us together in the heavenly places in Christ Jesus,

What an awesome God we serve! We are cleansed by His blood, made Holy by His blood and raised up by His Spirit to be One with Him. From this perspective of being seated with Christ, we can view the matters of human life very differently. We will not see the joys or the trials in the same we do on the earth. God can cause us to see His glory being manifest in us. God can show us the impact our lives have on those around us. We get knowledge and understanding of His ways and His purposes.

We do not have to be confined to a carnal human perspective of our lives. Positionally, Christ is seated on the Throne in heaven but He also is living inside of you and me and every Christian. Also, you are living in your human body but also, because of Christ, you are raised up into the Spiritual Body of Christ – the global Church – this is not just figurative language. You are part of His body – a member of Christ - seated with Christ on the Throne. You are a partaker with Him. We will rule and reign on the Earth. Once you realize this truth of Christ in you and you in Christ – literally- you will press into God to see the matters of your life from His vantage point in glory.

This does not take away from the present situation on Earth – the joys of human life or the pains of it. Rather – it lifts us above our human identities into the realm where all things are a part of God's higher purposes. What I used to literally do when things of Earth seemed to be overwhelming was literally get up on a chair and pray " God give me a new point of view. Help me to see things from your points of view." This physical act of faith demonstrated my spiritual yearning for God to show me a revelation of the situation I was in. He did it also. He would give me insight and wisdom beyond all natural understanding.

Proverbs 16: 3 Commit your works to the LORD,
and your thoughts will be established.

Are you planning something? Why not invite the LORD into the situation to get the most out of it. Invite God to manifest His presence and give you wisdom in everything that you do. As a child, I was involved in many sports. At these organized sporting events, there would be a prayer thanking God and inviting His presence. We also would say a pledge to Canada. Also, in school, we would pray together every day. Often there would be a scripture read. It gave us a sense of unity. It taught us respect for God. I didn't know God but I understood we were to be respectful. At public events – even at the movies, we stood for our national anthem and the LORD's prayer and God Save the Queen.

I believe that those minor parts of my life were as precious seed that God planted in my life so that I would desire to know Him. I know that was long ago and things change. I don't believe this is a good change. As we commit our ways to God in all things, He can protect, guide and give us His blessing.

Can You Let Go

Are you doing your life in your own strength? You could commit your job, your hobbies, your events, your home life, your friendships etc. to God. You could " cast the care of them" over on to God so that would care for you. You won't worry; you won't fret; you will be peaceful; you will be rejoicing. You won't be swayed by the facts – such as news reports or negative predictions. You will be able to maintain your peace because you will be living in the Spirit – God's Spirit will fill your spirit – in all aspects of your life.

Instead of worrying that you have not made your sales quota that day or that week, you will thank God for His provision. Roll the care of it over on to God; start praying God let me serve the customers with excellence. Let me be the best possible employee. God give me favour with customers; bring them to me. Literally, you will receive what you are believing and confessing.

Psalm 55: 22 Cast your burden on the LORD,
and He will sustain you;
He will never allow
the righteous to be moved.

Jesus cares for you in a way that is unique. Yes. He died for all people; but specifically, He died for you personally. He knew what you would do – all the good, all the bad, all the goofy and all of the sins. Jesus died for you knowing what you were and choosing to pay the price for your eternal salvation. He showed His love for you by His sacrifice. There is no one else you can trust with the things dearest to your heart; God cares for you. You can cast your cares over on to Him – knowing He will truly care for you. He cares for you more than you care for your own self.

If you are overwhelmed with care, pray. Get some prayer help also. If you know people who will pray for you, please give them your prayer request. If you don't have Christian friends. you know who you can trust with your prayer requests– send the requests to reputable ministries. There are thousands of Apostles, Prophets, Evangelists, Pastor, Teachers in North America. You can submit prayer request by letter or phone or on line. Those people will pray with you giving you the spiritual support that you need.

Casting your cares means you give it as you would a physical object. You had it but you gave it to God. Now He has it and He will care for you.

# 8 THE PRAYER OF PRAISE AND WORSHIP

Praying with all types of prayer in the supplication of the Holy Spirit includes the prayer of praise and worship. Many people think of these as separate than prayer but when we praise or worship, God is the audience so it is a type of prayer.

Psalm 100: 4 Enter his gates with thanksgiving
and his courts with praise;
give thanks to him and praise his name.

I taught on this scripture in a previous teaching. It explains the manner of praise and worship and the progression from thanksgiving, through praise and worship. It can be likened to the Temple at Jerusalem – the outer court being the place of thanksgiving; the Holy place being the place of praise; the most Holy place or Holy of Holies as the most sacred place of worship.

This pattern is an earthly example of the Heavenly reality. God gave Moses this pattern for the Tabernacle in the wilderness. He gave David this plan for the Temple that Solomon would build.

There is a progression in entrance into more intimate communion with God. In Heaven, God is seated on the Throne in the Holy of Holies. Only someone without sin can enter the Holy of Holies. What used to occur in the Old Testament was people would bring animals as sacrifice to cover their sin. The people never had access into the Holy of Holies. Their sins were not blotted out but they were covered by the sacrifice of an animal's blood – awaiting the day that Messiah would come. Jesus fulfilled this prophecy.

Because of Jesus' blood shed for us, we can enter into the presence of the most High God – in the Holiest place – speaking to God as a friend. We don't have to sacrifice animals; we can enter with boldness because Jesus paid the price for our Salvation. We offer spiritual sacrifices such as prayer, thanksgiving, praise and worship.

The Temple of the Holy Spirit

1 Peter 2: 5 you also, like living stones, are being built into a spiritual house[a]

to be a holy priesthood, offering spiritual sacrifices acceptable to God through Jesus Christ.

This scripture describes us as living members or stones in a spiritual temple. First, we are living or quickened by the Holy Spirit; we as members of the Body of Christ joined together to be a habitation of worship or a corporate Temple – we are the stones that create it. A different scripture calls us the Body of Christ.

1 Corinthians 12: 4 For just as each of us has one body with many members, and these members do not all have the same function, 5 so in Christ we, though many, form one body, and each member belongs to all the others. 6

In both these analogies, the corporate structure – members of the Body of Christ coming together, are more than the sum of their parts. By the living stones gathering together – we are not just stones but a spiritual Temple – a dwelling place for God. As individual members of the Body of Christ, we form a complete local Body of Christ. It can be as small as 2 or 3 members to a huge congregation of millions of people.

I Will Praise

The prayer of praise and worship starts with an act of human will. You decide to praise and worship God. As you might decide to go to a place or to do an activity, you humanly will to praise God. There are places where the Holy Spirit is moving and you literally feel like worshipping God. It is awesome. But you don't only praise or worship when you feel like it. You must make the decision and do it until you feel like it.

The reason is we don't always feel spiritually – you must stir up the gift of faith within yourself and release it by faith. You must start thanking God. God will always meet you as you in faith reach towards Him. I had a Pastor who used to dance before the LORD every service. He would will himself to praise and worship God no matter what else was going on. If things were going well, he danced before the LORD; if things were not going well, he danced before the LORD. He set a standard for all of us in that church. You praise and worship God because He is God – because He is worthy to be praised.

Hebrews Chapter 9 describes the Temple in Heaven. It talks about the things of the earth being a shadow of the Heavenly. Hebrews compares the earthly realm and our worship compared to the Heavenly realm and what exists in Heaven. It compares the Old Testament or covenant to the New Testament or new covenant. The following scripture shows how Christ made the way for us to enter the Holiest of all.

Hebrews 9: 14 How much more, then, will the blood of Christ, who through the eternal Spirit offered himself unblemished to God, cleanse our consciences from acts that lead to death,[c] so that we may serve the living God!

Because Jesus' blood washes us, cleanses us, makes us as though we have never sinned, we are made Holy by faith in Jesus Christ. We must believe this if we are to approach God's throne with boldness.

Why is Holiness so Important?

In the Old testament people had to offer sacrifices for their sins. Jesus paid the price once and for all by His death, burial and resurrection from the dead. Jesus blood does not cover our sins; it makes us as if we have never sinned. Often we Christians don't remember the immense privilege it is that we can praise or worship. What literally occurs is that as we determine with our will to thank God and praise and worship, our spirit offers spiritual sacrifices to God – we enter the Holy place of God in Heaven; as we worship, we enter into the Holiest of all. We are no longer cut off from God. We have access into the most Holy place in Heaven. God, who is Holy, engages with our spirit and we are One with the Creator of all things.
Prayer Chapter 8  Praise and worship

Praying with all types of prayer in the supplication of the Holy Spirit includes the prayer of praise and worship. Many people think of these as separate than prayer but when we praise or worship, God is the audience so it is a type of prayer.

Psalm 100: 4 Enter his gates with thanksgiving
and his courts with praise;
give thanks to him and praise his name.

I taught on this scripture in a previous teaching. It explains the manner of praise and worship and the progression from thanksgiving, through praise and worship. It can be likened to the Temple at Jerusalem – the outer court being the place of thanksgiving; the Holy place being the place of praise; the most Holy place or Holy of Holies as the most sacred place of worship.

This pattern is an earthly example of the Heavenly reality. God gave Moses this pattern for the Tabernacle in the wilderness. He gave David this plan for the Temple that Solomon would build.

There is a progression in entrance into more intimate communion with God. In Heaven, God is seated on the Throne in the Holy of Holies. Only someone without sin can enter the Holy of Holies. What used to occur in the Old Testament was people would bring animals as sacrifice to cover their sin. The people never had access into the Holy of Holies. Their sins were not blotted out but they were covered by the sacrifice of an animal's blood – awaiting the day that Messiah would come. Jesus fulfilled this prophecy.

Because of Jesus' blood shed for us, we can enter into the presence of the most High God – in the Holiest place – speaking to God as a friend. We don't have to sacrifice animals; we can enter with boldness because Jesus paid the price for our Salvation. We offer spiritual sacrifices such as prayer, thanksgiving, praise and worship.

The Temple of the Holy Spirit

1 Peter 2: 5 you also, like living stones, are being built into a spiritual house[a] to be a holy priesthood, offering spiritual sacrifices acceptable to God through Jesus Christ.

This scripture describes us as living members or stones in a spiritual temple. First, we are living or quickened by the Holy Spirit; we as members of the Body of Christ joined together to be a habitation of worship or a corporate Temple – we are the stones that create it. A different scripture calls us the Body of Christ.

1 Corinthians 12: 4 For just as each of us has one body with many members, and these members do not all have the same function, 5 so in Christ we, though many, form one body, and each member belongs to all the others. 6

In both these analogies, the corporate structure – members of the Body of Christ coming together, are more than the sum of their parts. By the living stones gathering together – we are not just stones but a spiritual Temple – a dwelling place for God. As individual members of the Body of Christ, we form a complete local Body of Christ. It can be as small as 2 or 3 members to a huge congregation of millions of people.

I Will Praise

The prayer of praise and worship starts with an act of human will. You decide to praise and worship God. As you might decide to go to a place or to do an activity, you humanly will to praise God. There are places where the Holy Spirit is moving and you literally feel like worshipping God. It is awesome. But you don't only praise or worship when you feel like it. You must make the decision and do it until you feel like it.

The reason is we don't always feel spiritually – you must stir up the gift of faith within yourself and release it by faith. You must start thanking God. God will always meet you as you in faith reach towards Him. I had a Pastor who used to dance before the LORD every service. He would will himself to praise and worship God no matter what else was going on. If things were going well, he danced before the LORD; if things were not going well, he danced before the LORD. He set a standard for all of us in that church. You praise and worship God because He is God – because He is worthy to be praised.

Hebrews Chapter 9 describes the Temple in Heaven. It talks about the things of the earth being a shadow of the Heavenly. Hebrews compares the earthly realm and our worship compared to the Heavenly realm and what exists in Heaven. It compares the Old Testament or covenant to the New Testament or new covenant. The following scripture shows how Christ made the way for us to enter the Holiest of all.

Hebrews 9: 14 How much more, then, will the blood of Christ, who through the eternal Spirit offered himself unblemished to God, cleanse our consciences from acts that lead to death,[c] so that we may serve the living God!

Because Jesus' blood washes us, cleanses us, makes us as though we have never sinned, we are made Holy by faith in Jesus Christ. We must believe this if we are to approach God's throne with boldness.

Why is Holiness so Important?

In the Old testament people had to offer sacrifices for their sins. Jesus paid the price once and for all by His death, burial and resurrection from the dead. Jesus blood does not cover our sins; it makes us as if we have never sinned. Often we Christians don't remember the immense privilege it is that we can praise or worship. What literally occurs is that as we determine with our will to thank God and praise and worship, our spirit offers spiritual sacrifices to God – we enter the Holy place of God in Heaven; as we worship, we enter into the Holiest of all. We are no longer cut off from God. We have access into the most Holy place in Heaven. God, who is Holy, engages with our spirit and we are One with the Creator of all things.

In the Old Testament, the people were always conscious of their sins; Jesus Christ cleansed us so we are Holy. The New covenant of Christ makes us Holy; this gives us boldness to approach God rather than to be fearful of Him. We are welcomed by God. We can offer up thanksgiving and praise.

Thanksgiving

Start thanking God first. Thank Him for saving you. Thank Him for what He has done for you. Never let your salvation be stale. How thankful am I that God saved me? I am eternally thankful. All of eternity I will thank God for reaching towards me to draw me to Himself. Once you start thanking God for what He has done for you, you could never stop thanking Him.

Has the LORD answered your prayers? Thank Him. Has God healed you? Thank Him. Has God delivered you? Thank Him. You cannot be a Christian very long without God blessing you. He will bless you physically, financially, spiritually, etc. He delights in giving us His best because His love for us is so strong that He would come to earth as a man (Jesus), live a Holy life and be put to death on a cross for our sins. He would rise from the dead giving us the victory over sin, hell and death if we would believe in Him.

Did God save some members of your family? Start thanking God for it. I cannot describe to you the joy in my life when my mother accepted Christ as her Saviour and LORD and got baptized in the Holy Spirit. I was so joyful, I literally dropped on my knees thanking God. I kept weeping because of the answer to my prayers. I was so overcome with joy, I could hardly speak. If you know me at all, you will know that very rarely am I without speech. That night at Church the pastor asked me how I felt. I was crying and speechless. He made a joke that it must have been a miracle that made me speechless.

Cultivate a heart of thanksgiving for what God does for you each day. Try to thank God for each moment you have on earth. He gives you each day that you have. Make it a point to thank God for each day. Thank God for your life, your food, your shelter, your family, your job. If we stopped at that place, you have a life superior to more than 2/3 the people on the planet. Thank God for your life – people who have near death experiences often get strong faith and commitment to God and are more expressively thankful for their lives.

Praise

Praise God for what He has done for you. Thank Him because He is God. As we thank God, we will begin to praise Him. Thanking Him is the act of will. You remember what He has done for you and you thank Him. As you thank Him, you begin to praise Him with personalized praise or with choruses. You could simply start saying with all your heart meaning it " I praise you Jesus." As you continue to focus on praising Him, it begins to flow like a facet flowing. The praise keep releasing more praises.

God inhabits the praises of His people. God comes and His presence increases in us as we praise and worship Him. Praise to God starts flowing from your spirit. The best way for me to describe praise is priming the pump. Literally start some wells of water by pouring some water into the pump. It starts the mechanism so that water begins to flow. The thanksgiving is the primer and as you being to praise God, it is your spirit magnifying God in a flow. As you are praising God – His Spirit fills you. It lifts you, releases joy and more thanksgiving and praise. His Spirit fills your spirit.

Scripture instructs us how to praise God – continuously as in Hebrews 13: 15 Through Jesus, therefore, let us continually offer to God a sacrifice of praise—the fruit of lips that openly profess his name. 16 And do not forget to do good and to share with others, for with such sacrifices God is pleased.

As you are praising, you draw closer to God in worship. You will start praising God for things He is revealing to you in the present moment. You become so aware of His presence with you that you will want to express your love for Him with all your being. An expression of this overwhelming experience can be seen the woman who anointed Jesus with oil. She poured the most expensive thing she owned onto Jesus. She poured a rare, expensive, treasure upon Jesus to show her extravagant love for Him. The disciples didn't understand why she did it. Jesus knew she was giving her all- in worship to Him.

Matthew 26: 6 While Jesus was in Bethany in the home of Simon the Leper, 7 a woman came to him with an alabaster jar of very expensive perfume, which she poured on his head as he was reclining at the table.

Judas commented that they could have sold such a precious thing for money. He did not understand the worship because he was only thinking of money. Lucifer was the praise and worship leader in Heaven. He covered the throne of God – giving the praises of creation to God. Sin was within him because he decided to keep part of the praise for himself and not give it to God. That is when he got thrown out of heaven. He lost his place because of pride – not giving God the glory that is due to God only.

In the New testament, Herod the king, boasted about himself and died immediately after proclaiming himself to be as god.

Acts 12: 21 On the appointed day Herod, wearing his royal robes, sat on his throne and delivered a public address to the people. 22 They shouted, "This is the voice of a god, not of a man." 23 Immediately, because Herod did not give praise to God, an angel of the Lord struck him down, and he was eaten by worms and died.

All glory belongs to God only. There is only one God and He is worthy of all praise, honour and glory. As we praise God, we are magnifying Him and giving Him glory. Jesus blood shed for us gives us access to the Holiest of all. Never take your access to the most Holy God lightly. There are different expressions of our praise and worship: dancing, weeping, crying, shouting – all types of expressions of our praise and worship.

Worship is complete oneness with God. It is assuming the posture or position of worship. It doesn't mean your physical body alone. Inside your innermost being, you are giving God all that you are. It is total abandonment to God. You give your spirit, soul and body wholly to God. It is like the woman who poured the anointment on Jesus and wiped his feet with her hair. She showed her total giving of herself to God – this is what worship is. There is no separation – there is only Oneness.

International House of Prayer Kansas City

Something like this is being done at International House of Prayer in Kansas City Missouri. The church worships God day and night 24/7 - 365 days a year. There are certain prayer rooms where people are praising, worshipping, praying constantly (since 1999). Some people might see this as a waste, because the people are making many sacrifices of their lives to pray, praise and worship. This is an extravagant offering – giving of their lives literally to praise and worship God as the Levites did in the Old Testament.

Please know that these people do works of social justice, evangelism, missions, but they also give themselves wholly to praise and worship. They are pouring out their lives unto Jesus. Some people at that church attend the church and have jobs and other activities; some of them, collect donations of money to finance themselves to full time praise and worship and prayer and ministry. That is their main passion and what they give themselves to.

## Levitical Priesthood

The Levite priests were chosen by God as the one tribe of 12 to praise, worship and serve the LORD in ministry. They made sacrifices; they cared for the Temple; they offered incense; they lived wholly unto God.

Praise and worship should be a regular part of a Christian's life. Yes of course the corporate church but also in our own lives. Appoint a time for yourself to pray, praise and worship. Keep it as important time with God daily. Make it your choice each day. Make God your first choice each day. Is He your first choice?

When worship happens in a congregation, people will go to their knees to praise God. Some people may lie on the ground prostrate before God. The holiness of God is so magnificent and overwhelming that the people cannot stand or even kneel – they lie face down trembling in God's presence. There is weeping, because there is intensity of the pleasure of the awesomeness of God. Have you ever been in a meeting where the presence of God is so strong that your knees are shaking because of the presence of God upon you? If you haven't pray – O God reveal your glory realms to me. Pray for revival at your church. People who give themselves wholly to God in worship know the awesomeness of His presence.

## The Presence of God Ignites Faith

Through praise and worship, the presence of God comes mightily. Faith is ignited and people can receive healing. I want to tell you about what happened to me. I had sprained my ankle. It was swollen and it was sore. I went to church anyway. The presence of God was there so strong that I heard a voice that said "Can you believe?" I literally said yes I believe and started dancing on that foot. I was dancing and there was no pain. I sang and danced with all my might. I was completely healed by the presence of the LORD in the praise and worship. The people had a desire to worship God. The atmosphere was strong joyful praise. I thanked God with all my being.

## Gifts of the Spirit Manifest

Often the gift of prophecy starts to flow when there is praise and worship. Prophets in the Old Testament would often ask a minstrel to play an instrument before they prophesied. King David, used to play the harp, and he wrote many of the psalms to God that are prophetic praise. All the psalm writers were worshipping God with their songs. As the prophets of God began to worship, the Spirit of God began to move and they were moved to prophesy. Praise and worship and prophecy are connected. The manifest presence of GOD Is necessary for the gifts of the Spirit to flow. The gifts of the Spirit will begin all over the sanctuary as the presence of God is strong. People may not even know why but they will go to the altar and kneel and pray and weep and rededicate their lives to God.

The Presence of God is Attractive

I have been in a church where this type of presence of God moved throughout the church on a Sunday – week after week after week. There was a couple who were driving by and felt a strong urge to come into the building. They came in during praise and worship. They went down to the altar and kneeled and prayed. They were not even Christians. They stayed there all throughout the praise and worship and received Jesus as their Saviour and gave their testimony that they felt compelled to come into the church building. I believe the anointing was so strong, it drew them in like a magnet draws metal.

To get into the realm of the miraculous, you have got to be praising and worshipping God with all your being. God's presence comes – but is not for no reason. It is always for a purpose. God will save, heal, deliver; miracles can occur. As worshippers who feel God's presence, they will experience ignited faith or a faith boost that will help them direct their faith at target needs. Whatever you have need of, God is the answer. In the atmosphere of praise and worship, people will dance, will shout, will run around the church, will lie prostrate on the ground, will kneel will laugh, will cry etc. The presence of God comes of the people and they rec3ive whatever they have need of.

God Inhabits the Praises of His People

If you want a miracle or need an answer to prayer, start worshipping God. His presence will come and you will receive. He may give you instruction or speak to you. Often He will speak scriptures to me that I later read and receive wisdom from.

Worship is abandonment to God. It is giving all your spirit, soul and body unto God. You give all you are to God that He might fill you with Himself. Sometimes His Holiness is so overwhelming that you can`t even lift up your head because you are aware of His Holy presence there in you. You may weep or silently gasp in awe of His presence. You can be so at ONE with God your body is literally quivering. Your spirit hovers inside of you.

The presence of God is to be desired more than anything on this earth because we were created to worship; God will instruct us, teach us, fill us, heal us, use us. Often in these types of meetings, God will instruct someone to go pray for someone else or to speak a word of encouragement to someone. The purpose for drawing in is because He is God. You desire Him and you are filled with Him. The pleasure of His presence cannot be described in early terms.

If you only go to God to ask something from Him, you don`t have it. You don`t have the revelation of how special your relationship with God is. Once you realize the holiness and overwhelming love of God towards you and you connect with Him, you will want to seek Him simply to worship and praise Him. You will ask God to use you to minister to others. You will present yourself a living sacrifice.

John 4: 21 Jesus said to her, "Woman, believe Me, the hour is coming when neither on this mountain nor in Jerusalem will you worship the Father. 22 You worship what you do not know; we know what we worship, for salvation is of the Jews. 23 Yet the hour is coming, and is now here, when the true worshippers will worship the Father in spirit and truth. For the Father seeks such to worship Him. 24 God is Spirit, and those who worship Him must worship Him in spirit and truth."

Jesus ministers to the woman of the well in Samaria because he knows everything about her. He gives her these words knowing all the other aspects of her life, including her sins, are symptoms of what she really needs: that is how to connect with the One true God. His words penetrate her hard shell and Jesus reveals Himself to her as the Messiah. She realizes that He has told her secret things of her heart. She realizes He is the Messiah and she runs into town, evangelizing by saying come and see a man who told me all things about my life.

Worship God throughout Your Day

We should have a heart with an inclination to prayer and worship constantly. You may be doing a secular job, but your heart is fixed on Jesus and you are asking Him to help you do your best. If you are stuck in traffic, you can be praising and worshipping God. You will be totally free no matter what your situation is. You will be rejoicing because God is with you and His presence is strong. Start by setting your will to worship. I will to worship you Jehovah. Begin thanking Him and praising Him. You can be here on earth and in the Holy of Holies in heaven simultaneously aware of both. You can live in your spirit rather than in your soul.

God can Speak to You in Praise

Praise begins when we fix our hearts on God and praising Him with no other agenda. During praise and worship, God may give words of wisdom to you. You didn`t go to Him to get something but your needs ae met anyway. There was a man who was an engineer and trying to create huge mining trucks. He was trying to solve an issue for days but could not. He decided to go to church Sunday rather than stay home with his work. As he began to praise God during the service – God revealed the solution to the issue about the huge trucks. He was faithfully serving God and God knowing what he had need of – gave it to him. My pastor told me about this situation. Creative solutions can come as you are praising and worshipping God.

Enter His Presence

If you are a spirit filled Christian, you have access to the presence of God and the privileges of a Christian. You know I have a key chain with many keys. Some of those keys I use every day. Some I don`t. As a child of God, you have the key to enter into God`s presence. Do you want to enter? You can choose to enter in, but some people although they have access don`t. They do not try to enter the Holy of Holies with God. You can have as much of God as you want. If you do not want more of God, He will never force Himself on you.

An example of someone who embraces God's Presence is Mary the mother of Jesus. The angel appears and reveals a prophecy to her about her being pregnant with Jesus. She says Be it unto me according to your will. She surrenders herself to God. She is a special woman because she gave herself in agreement with the prophecy by the angel. She received it as God's Word.

Peace in Hos Presence

In praise and worship no demon can stay. As you press into God, demons cannot enter into the Holy place of God. Because I was not raised as a Christian. I did not know what peace was for most of my life. In the congregation at church I would feel the anointing of the LORD during praise and worship and I would feel God s peace. I thought it had to do with the church itself. I would desire to be in the services. God impressed on me that I did not have to wait to worship God during church but I could begin to praise and worship God every day. As I obeyed this prompting, I realized that peace would come as a result of my praise and worship and also God would speak to me and lead me in my daily life. When you are in the presence of God, there is perfect peace. You know it. There is nothing to compare it to on earth.

I started with small things like thanking God for worship service, thanking Him for my school, my job, my day. As I began, praise began to come and next worship. Soon, it was flowing in joy and peace and I was seeing things differently from God s point of view. I literally saw the fulfillment of this scripture. The oil of joy and rejoicing so strong that the presence of the LORD was overwhelming me with light – revelation, insight. I could see situations on earth from a Heavenly point of view.

Isaiah 61: to preserve those who mourn in Zion,
to give to them beauty
for ashes,
the oil of joy
for mourning,
the garment of praise
for the spirit of heaviness,
that they might be called trees of righteousness,
the planting of the LORD,
that He might be glorified.

I put on a garment of praise. I literally chose to praise and starting doing it until praises started bubbling up from my innermost being. You can choose to put on praise and worship. Sometimes you won' t want to stop praising and worshipping. If you need to, set a timer so you will know when to stop so you can go about the very day aspects of your life. You will do it with more zeal because your spirit is encouraged. Usually songs will come into your spirit and you will begin singing throughout the day – your spirit singing with the Holy Spirit.

I do not worship God to get something, but I always receive something from Him while I worship Him. Remember to add in some thanksgiving for what He has done for you, for filling you. Thank God for your life on earth.

# 9 PRAYER OF AGREEMENT

Matthew 18:19 "Again I say to you, that if two of you agree on earth about anything they ask, it will be done for them by My Father who is in heaven. 20 For where two or three are assembled in My name, there I am in their midst."

In this scripture, the truth that two are stronger than one is revealed. Jesus says that his presence will be with us of 2 or more of us gather in agreement. Yes, He is living inside each one of us but as we gather together, His Holy presence is in a new dynamic. There is a multiplication of strength as Christians gather together. One of us can put a thousand to flight; 2 of us can put 10, 000 to flight. Two agreeing in faith is so important. Jesus is our high priest who is making intercession for us. He also is praying for us. He joins with us as we pray in agreement.

Prayer Partner

Do you have a special friend that you can pray with about important things? You cannot pray in agreement with just anyone. If the person does not agree with you in spirit and in the particular matter you are praying about, you will not be equally yoked. You must be of the same spirit and you must also agree in prayer about the matter. If two agree, that means both must be in unity. You cannot take this scripture by itself though. Please get all the teachings in this series – what you are praying for cannot be against God's will. It must agree with God's expressed will which is His written Word.

For example, you can't pray for a man to divorce his wife and marry you. That is clearly against God's Word. Should these thoughts come to you at all, and you would want to pray them, you must get some teaching from the Word of God on what God likes and doesn't like. If you know it is a sin but you desire it anyway, you require deliverance. You can't pray for things against the laws of earth or against the laws of heaven.

Spiritual Friends

The type of friend I am talking about is a true child of God – somebody who knows God's Word and you could take communion with him or her and you could both say you agree on the scriptures as the Word of God. We believe the only atonement for our sin is Jesus blood. You believe the Word of God is without error. You believe it is the expressed will of God. You can agree on the doctrines of Christ. Listen, even if no one in your family is saved, you can have a friend in faith. You are never alone. There is always somebody who will come into agreement with you.

Christian Media

Christian media connects us to real Christians who will pray for you and agree with you in prayer about important matters. There are so many awesome media ministries that you can request prayer from. On the Internet, there are hundreds of reputable ministries that would be glad to pray for you and with you. I can personally share how valuable these ministries are, because I have had periods where there is no one else to agree with me in prayer – but there is always the body of Christ Universal. There are always ministries that would be glad to pray for you.

Get Someone to Agree on the Important Things.

It is worth it to write your prayer request or type it or phone the ministry. Having someone else agree with you in prayer is essential. It is so important that you treasure the true Christian friends you do have and encourage each other spiritually through prayer and words of encouragement from the scriptures. Always remember that Jesus is sitting on the throne in agreement with you. Jesus blood poured upon the mercy seat is speaking for you from Heaven – proclaiming your holiness.

Part of our Christian friendships should always include prayer, praise, communion, devotional discussion.

The Early Church

Acts 4: 32 All the believers were of one heart and one soul, and no one said that what he possessed was his own. But to them all things were in common. 33 With great power the apostles testified to the resurrection of the Lord Jesus, and great grace was on them all. 34 There was no one among them who lacked, for all those who were owners of land or houses sold them, and brought the income from what was sold, 3

Gathering

They would gather together every day praying and remembering the

LORD and having communion and supper together. The early Church met in homes of the people. They gathered praying for one another and caring for each other. The actual disciples in each other's homes is how this gospel spread from family to family. They came into agreement.

Giving

They were in such agreement that they shared and no one went without. If someone had a need, someone else would join in and give. They literally gave of their possessions so no one went without. No one told them they had to; they knew it was right to give to those who needed; they loved each other as they loved their own selves.

The prayer of agreement requires knowledge of the will of God, and agreement in spirit and faith expressed together.

1.  You may have to search the scriptures to find what God says about the topic.
2.  You may have to speak with your friend to know his or her heart concerning the matter.
3.  You must both agree with faith expressed so that the release of your faith will release angels to go about performing the answer to prayer.

Search the Scriptures

A concordance is an excellent resource. Most people use the electronic ones now – but if you would type in the topic you want scriptures about into a website such as Bible gateway, you would see hundreds of scriptures in the results section.

There are books of scriptures – usually called titles like promises for women or promises about prosperity etc. Joyce Meyer has an excellent book entitled The Power of God's Word. It has sections of topics where people may need prayer and scriptures underneath each section. Praying the Word of God is quoting God to God. If it is in the Word of God, you know it is God's will. He gave us the Word of God so we could know how to pray and how to live on earth. For example, this scripture:

Philippians 4: 19 19 But my God shall supply your every need according to His riches in glory by Christ Jesus.

God will supply all our needs according to His riches in glory. First, God cares about our needs. He promises to supply them. Because He will supply them according to His riches (not ours) you know He can never run out. The known will of God here is that God will care for your needs. He will always supply. You must also know the scripture: Mark 11: 24 Therefore I say to you, whatever things you ask when you pray, believe that you will receive them, and you will have them.

Ask in Faith

If you do not ask God for your need, you may not receive anything. You must ask Him even though He knows you have need of it, because He wants us to trust Him and to know He is our source of supply. The prayer of agreement requires knowledge of the scriptures on the topic you are praying about. Search the scriptures concerning your need whether it be health, prosperity, a bill paid, a new car etc. Even though you will not find a scripture that says God wants you to have a new car, you will see that if you need a car, God wants to supply it.

We should invest in some of those scripture books. I have several of these scripture books organized by topic. I also have scriptures I've written on index cards. I put one scripture on each card. They are important things I want in my life. I pray them over myself. I pray them over others. It is also important to get into Bible studies and cell groups or places where we discuss scripture and learn about what God's Word declares. The more we learn God's Word, the more we learn how to pray about situations.

Agreeing with Somebody

Secondly, it requires knowing the spirit of the person you are praying for. That is discerning in the spirit, the need of the person, and the direction of the leading of the Holy Spirit. Your friend may have a scripture for you. Your friend may discern some other aspect. That is why it is so important to have spiritual friends.

Christian Ministries often hire people to pray over prayer requests. Not only do the ministers themselves but staff members etc. Some minsters such as Benny Hinn, pray for them, have his staff pray for them, and then send them to a prayer room in Jerusalem so they can be prayed for in Israel. If you do not have a close Christian friend to pray with you in agreement, please consider some of the reputable Christian Ministries who offer this as a service to Christ praying over prayer requests.

We are the body of Christ in the earth. We can minster much by agreeing in faith with friends. Should you be discipling someone, always include in your conversation, Is there anything I can pray with you about?

Out Reach

One of my delights in life has to been a prayer counsellor or altar worker. It means standing at the altar and praying for and with people who have special prayer requests. I knew this in a sort of informal way at one of my churches where I wasn't given a title but the Holy Spirit prompted me and I started going to the altar to pray for people. There were no appointed prayer workers; there were people who cared who came forward to kneel beside people and pray with them.

In a couple of my churches we were given a badge with our name on it and the church name and we stood in the altar area waiting for people to approach. Often what I would ask them was Is there something I can pray about with you? The 700 Club – Pat Robertson has an excellent manual of prayer scriptures for their phone prayer teams with huge sections of scriptures on all types of topics.

At one of my churches we used the prayer of agreement as an outreach. It was near Christmas so we went door to door giving a token gift and church information. We would ask Is there anything I can pray about with you? Some people said no politely and tried to offer us money. We received no money from anyone on purpose. Some people would say no politely and shut the door. I was lucky; we never had any rude people. At some homes the person answered yes please. I faced people in tears; homes with family fights going on etc. During these prayers, I felt peace imparted to those people. They knew somebody cared. They knew somebody believed in God. Those two statements sometimes make all the difference in someone's life.

Unity of Believers

Psalm 133: 2 It is like precious oil upon the head,
that runs down on the beard—
even Aaron's beard—
and going down to the collar of his garments;
3 as the dew of Hermon,
that descends upon the mountains of Zion,
for there the LORD has commanded the blessing,
even life forever.

In this scripture, the description of unity among the congregation of believers is described as the anointing oil of God poured upon Aaron the high priest. He was chosen by God, anointed by God and it was symbolic in the anointing oil. That oil was fragrant. It was made special by God's command. It was to anoint the ministers as they entered the Holy of Holies. The blessing or favour of God was upon him to serve God and pray for the people. The scripture describes it as the place where God commands the blessing.

It is in this type of joining together in prayer, with someone of like precious faith, that God responds to the prayer of agreement. God expresses His pleasure in those who dwell in unity of faith.

Caution

If you cannot come into agreement with someone about a prayer request – state that you can`t. Don`t pretend that you do. Let me give you an example. I was a new Christian, I was expecting to win a contest for 1 million dollars. It required no money .I entered my name. I asked people to pray with me that I would win this contest. I could not find anyone who would agree with me about this topic. It is not forbidden by scripture. I did not believe it wrong to enter the contest. I had certain charities on my heart and I wanted to help myself and my family. At that point in my Christian life, I did not know about writing prayer requests to other ministries. A mature Christian could have prayed with me. Perhaps he or she may have discerned my heart – but it is best if you can not agree – to say No I can`t agree.

If you pretend to pray with someone, such as saying the words of agreement but you don`t agree, you are sinning against God and that person. If you cannot agree, you must say so. If there is a scriptural reason, you should state it. If it is your opinion – say so.

Never let someone pray for you if you do not agree with what they are praying – pull away and say `I cannot agree with this.` If you sense anything in your spirit that is not in agreement with God`s Word, pull away and state out loud : I do not agree with this`. It matters in Heaven. It matters in the atmosphere`s of the earth. It is not usually an issue at church but is could be and you should be aware of it.

The Importance of the Body of Christ

1 Corinthians 12: 4 There are various gifts, but the same Spirit. 5 There are differences of administrations, but the same Lord. 6 There are various

operations, but it is the same God who operates all of them in all people.

In this chapter, the Apostle Paul discusses the importance of spiritual gifts and the body of Christ like a human body with comparison to the hands, the eyes etc. The scripture states that a body only functions properly as it works together. If I want something – my brain sends a signal to my hand to reach for it to take it. If I wants to go someplace, my brain send signals throughout my body so I can get up and go to the place. The body functioning properly is what is ideal. It requires total harmony or unity. If one part isn`t functioning, believe me you know about it.

I have known several people who have either broken or sprained their smallest toe. First of all the people say they never realized how much they used that seemingly insignificant part of their body. They walk, they move, they bang it – pain. They didn`t realize its value, until it wasn`t functioning properly. It is also like this in the body of Christ. If one part is not functioning properly or not in agreement with the other parts, it affects the whole body.

Restoring the Broken

If a member of the church is cut off from the rest of the church, we must do whatever we can to remedy this situation. We should do our best to reach towards a person to rejoin or connect with him or her. This includes caring for each other; praying for each other and making attempts to reconnect people.

I`ve had several such opportunities. Usually a person got offended, stopped coming to church and stayed home. Sometimes, that person went elsewhere. What was happening in the spiritual realm is someone got wounded (because something was either said abruptly or wrongly or misconstrued) and on the inside that person was suffering. The person was no longer normal. Just as though it were a physical wound that would make you act differently, so was the spiritual wound; the person was acting strange. True love reaching out to people such as this. Speaking with him or her, praying with and for him and her and on some occasions more than once can result in restoring people to the local body they belong in.

You That are Spiritual

Galatians 6: 1 Brothers, if a man is caught in any transgression, you who are spiritual should restore such a one in the spirit of meekness, watching yourselves, lest you also be tempted. 2 Bear one another's burdens, and so fulfill the law of Christ.

To reach out to members who are not functioning properly, you should be meek, gentle, kind, sincere – filled with the Holy Spirit. You must genuinely care or it means nothing. You need God`s anointing and direction to speak to these people and pray with them. These people who reach out to others and pray with them and help them get reconnected are as frontline soldiers or ministers – bringing life to the Body of Christ.

Prayer of Binding and Loosing

This type of prayer is important but is not to be used lightly. It should be used with discernment.

Matthew 18:18 "Truly I say to you, whatever you bind on earth will be bound in heaven, and whatever you loose on earth will be loosed in heaven.
19 "Again I say to you, that if two of you agree on earth about anything they ask, it will be done for them by My Father who is in heaven. 20 For where two or three are assembled in My name, there I am in their midst."
In this type of prayer, two or more people agree upon something on earth that involves concerning the opening or shutting of doors in Heaven. It directly affects the spirit realm because there is a command to it where the forces of darkness are bound and the angels of God are released. God directs us by the Holy Spirit through words of wisdom and words of knowledge to stop certain things and release other things. They may seem ordinary but they are in fact spiritual in origin.

Usually a demonic force is discerned and bound and angels are released to bring Go's Word to come to pass. Example, if you discern in your spirit rebellion you would say out loud "I bind you spirit of rebellion. You cannot continue. Leave this place. God, release angels who will come protect NAME THE PERSON. Let there be humility and obedience." This is direct example of using it by the Holy Spirit.

# 10 THE PRAYER OF REPENTANCE

You would not have been able to come to Christ if it were not His love drawing you. You had to admit you were a sinner and you need a Saviour. What I have described is the first use of the gift of Repentance. It is a gift – that God softens your heart and makes you want to be cleansed from your sin. Only the presence of the Holy Spirit drawing you, motivating you to want more of God allows you to come. It is the magnetic pull of mercy from you to God.

Romans 10: 9 that if you confess with your mouth Jesus is Lord, and believe in your heart that God has raised Him from the dead, you will be saved, 10 for with the heart one believes unto righteousness, and with the mouth confession is made unto salvation.

God's mercy was drawing you so that you wanted to know more about Him. You wanted to know about spiritual things. You wanted to know God. You had to believe that Jesus died for your sins or you could not be a Christian. You must confess with your mouth that you believe this. Knowing that Jesus died for your sins means accepting His blood shed on Calvary for your life personally. You must believe it in a personal way. This profession of faith makes you a Christian.

Enmity

As soon as you were born on the earth, you were born a sinner. Because we inherited the sins of Adam and Eve's disobedience to God, there is a rebellion in us against God. We must accept Him as Saviour and receive the cleansing of blood to be free of this sin, often referred to as original sin. There are some sins we do ignorantly, the sins we do on purpose and the sins inherited through iniquity.

Sins we do in Ignorance

If we did not know what God desires and do things against His will – it is sin. You may not know it is a sin, but as soon as you find out the truth about it, you should repent, or confess that sin to God and ask Him for forgiveness.

Willful sin

If you know what God's Word is on a matter, and willfully go against it, it is willful sin. You are sinning on purpose. Whatever the sin itself is, it is combined with rebellion and disobedience to God. What must you do? There is a mercy God gives us, that if we sin, we feel Him tugging at the heart to return to Him. What you must do is run to Him. Ask God to forgive you for it. Ask for the cleansing of God for the sin. If you do not feel the tugging at your heart to return but have knowledge it is sin – pray for mercy that God would cause you to feel true repentance. Only God can give you the mercy of true repentance. You cannot in your own strength do it. If you know it is something you enjoy – literally plead the blood of Jesus over yourself and pray that you will love the things God loves and hate the things God hates.

God can and will give you the strength through Christ who lives in you to live above the fleshly realm of sin. But your human will does play a part – Turn to God rather than away from Him.

Turning to Him means you know you need a Saviour. You realize there is nothing in you that can do it. But the good news is that Jesus Christ lives within you.

Philippians 4: 13 I can do all things because of Christ who strengthens me.

The presence of the Holy Spirit can transform you. As you pray, as you confess God's word and pray God's word over yourself, God transforms you – just as a potter who is making a pot shapes the pot with his or her hands, as you pray, God is transforming you.

2 Corinthians 3: 18 But we all, seeing the glory of the Lord with unveiled faces, as in a mirror, are being transformed into the same image from glory to glory by the Spirit of the Lord.

Iniquities

There are sins that attach themselves to families. It is done by physical example (alcoholism often is passed on within families) but it is deeper. It also is passed on through the spirit. For instance you may know that a person is a liar. Someone tells you " all that family are liars'. We notice it in others but not always in ourselves.

Numbers 14: 18 'The LORD is slow to anger and abounding in mercy, forgiving iniquity and transgression; but He will by no means clear the guilty, visiting the iniquity of the fathers upon the children to the third and fourth generation.

Jeremiah 31: 30 But everyone will die for his own iniquity. Every man that eats the sour grape, his teeth will be set on edge.

Ezekiel 18: 20 The soul who sins shall die. The son shall not bear the punishment of the iniquity of the father, nor shall the father bear the punishment of the iniquity of the son. The righteousness of the righteous shall be upon himself, and the wickedness of the wicked shall be upon himself.

Jesus Forgives All Sin

The good news is that Jesus blood shed for you can wash away all types of sin. If you know that you are willfully sinning (and repenting and sinning again) ask God to reveal to you if it is a family sin. If there are others in your family heritage bound by those same sins, pray and ask God to have mercy on you and also your family. You can make the decision to cut off iniquity from your family. You can plead the blood of Jesus (pray for Jesus blood to cleanse you) over yourself and your children. It does not have to continue in your family. Start finding scriptures on that area – what God's word says about it – start confessing it – saying it and praying it over yourself and your family.

The prayer of repentance God initiates by giving you a prompting to come to Him. This gift of repentance will be with you all your life on earth. It is God's mercy towards you so that you can live without sin in your life. As soon as it comes to you, repent and ask for forgiveness.

It is important that you get strong teaching on the Blood of Jesus so that you know the same God that saved you, is the same God that can forgive you. He knew your sins when he died on the cross – all of them; He paid the price with His precious blood. The blood of Jesus makes you Holy – it is the righteousness of God in Christ. Jesus blood is sprinkled on the Mercy seat in Heaven. That blood speaks over your life – Holy.

1 John 1 : 9 If we confess our sins, He is faithful and just to forgive us our sins and cleanse us from all unrighteousness.

Jesus forgave us over 2000 years ago. Yes, you should ask for forgiveness but God already did it. It is a matter of you confessing and receiving. Never believe the lie that your sin can not be forgiven. Jesus died for all people past, present and future. It is an act of human will to ask for repentance. Make the decision.

You don't have to say it to a person unless God prompts you in your heart. If you have sinned against another person, you should also ask for his or her forgiveness after you confess to God. You have got to repent to God. He may place upon your heart people to speak to. It is not hard to do. It is an act of humility – to admit that you need a Saviour. We need a Saviour for all of our lives on earth and for all eternity. Jesus is the Saviour.

Forgiveness

As a teacher, I notice how close kids are with their parents because if they messed up something at school such as a poor grade or correction in behaviour, they will go running to their dad or their mum and tell them. This shows they know their parents love them without condition. They will confess what they have done and ask for forgiveness. It is the type of love I am speaking about. God loves you no matter what you have done. It is not okay to sin. It is not that God doesn't see the sin, but as soon as you ask for forgiveness, He blots it out as if you never sinned. God loves us unconditionally; God forgives us unconditionally.

I have known some Christians who cannot forgive themselves. They sin and they repent but then they go on blaming themselves for sin. This is totally un biblical. Once you confess your sin, you must receive the forgiveness of Jesus Christ in His death, burial and resurrection over 2000 years ago. Jesus forgave you with His life's blood. His last words were "It is finished." He considered done. You or I must come into agreement with Jesus. If you don't feel forgiven – get your feelings in alignment with God's Word. Start confessing scripture over yourself such as follows:

1 Corinthians 5: 21 God made Him who knew no sin to be sin for us, that we might become the righteousness of God in Him.

Start confessing I am the righteousness of God in Jesus Christ. Jesus shed His blood for me. I am Holy because of the blood of Jesus. Do not resist the mercy of the LORD Jesus Christ. God wants you to move on – to receive forgiveness and to go on living for Him. Start confessing I receive the forgiveness of sin. Pray and thank God for it.

In Acts 2, on the day of Pentecost, the disciples were filled with the Holy Spirit and were speaking in tongues. And went out into the streets speaking in tongues. Some people thought they were drunk and in response the

Apostle Peter preaches all the Messianic prophecies and how Jesus fulfilled them. He explains the gift of the Holy Spirit as a fulfillment of Joel 2: 28. Finally, he points the fingers at the religious crowd gathered and blames them for Jesus death (it was the Pharisees who handed him over to be crucified). They respond with a desperate cry of
What can we do? (Acts 2: 37)

Peter replies Acts 2:38 Repent and be baptized every one of you in the name of Jesus Christ for forgiveness of sins, and you shall receive the gift of the Holy Spirit.

If they could be forgiven who literally handed Jesus over to die by a painful death, how could there be anyone who cannot be forgiven? Jesus cried out on the cross "Forgive them for they know not what they do". With His dying words – Jesus was praying for us – praying forgiveness for us.

Are you Truly Forgiven When you Accept Christ?

You are truly forgiven and saved when you receive Jesus Christ as your Savior. But there is so much that must be changed inside of us that God continues a Holy work of sanctification in us throughout all our lives. What this means is, He will reveal by the Spirit things to cut out of your life. He never brings condemnation but there is a sense of the thing or activity or whatever is not pleasing to God and we will know we must get rid of it.

Testimony

In my own life, I was radically saved. I mean I was completely going in a different direction than God and in His mercy towards me He found a way to reach me. As I said my first prayer of repentance asking for eternal life, I felt a heavy stone was rolled off my being. I literally felt freedom. I was forgiven and I knew it. (whether you feel it or not you are forgiven). This is Justification – or the process of the application of Jesus blood to make us just as if we had never sinned.

But in my own life I had much cleaning to do. This is what I mean. The first year or years at Church I most spent crying and praying. It seemed that the Word of God taught and preached was directly piercing my innermost being every sermon. I would go to the altar and weep. Sometimes I would pray " O God show me how to hate what you hate and love what you love." Mostly I was realizing how Holy God is and how much I needed Him. If any sins came to me that I was doing, I confessed them. I wanted to live Holy for God. This process of God transforming us from glory to glory is called sanctification. It is God's mercy towards us, revealing things to us that are not pleasing to Him. The Holy Spirit never forces you to repent.

You could resist God – but the fact the Holy Spirit brings it to you, the way the Holy Spirit gently nudges you to repent – you realize God wants the best for you. Anything that could lead to sin, hell or death or harm to yourself, God wants to protect you from it. The reason God doesn't want you to do it is because He knows it will result in death. Sin always has a consequence. It separates us from God. It leads to destruction. My running to God as He softened my heart towards Him caused me to focus on Christ and what He did for me.

Give No Place to the Devil

I will give you an example of what I am talking about. I was exploring Eastern Religions and had gathered much jewelry that were of various gods and religious symbols of those Eastern religions. The day after receiving Christ, I felt the LORD impress on me to get rid of all the books on witchcraft and other gods. My first response was the cost of the books. God continued to impress it on me as important. I knew it was God. I gathered the stuff and burned it. Please know – I had no Christian upbringing. I had never read much of the Bible. I didn`t know what I was doing was scriptural. Soon after I spoke to the people who lead me to the LORD. They told me that it was in the Bible. In Acts 19: 19 it is recorded – the burning of witchcraft things.

I thought I was done getting rid of stuff. After excellent teaching on not giving any entry point for the devil, I realized that some things such as idols or graven images could be an entrance way for the enemy. I was doing something normal and suddenly it came to my mind that I had a scarab piece of jewelry that I had not thrown out. God revealed its exact location. I found it and threw it out. I obeyed the prompting of the Holy Spirit. This type of response to God revealing something unpleasing to Him is obedience and repentance.

No Idols or Graven Images

The commandments preach against idols or graven images. These things seem innocent in appearance, but they should not be found in a Christian's life. If you know, you clearly know it is wrong because of the Scriptures, you must get rid of it. If you do not clearly know, pray about it. Ask God to reveal to you clearly what to do. Let peace be the umpire. Say it out loud. `I am going to keep this unless you prompt me otherwise. Holy

Spirit, if it is wrong, convict me `If you are willing to obey God, that is what God desires. He will never not answer you. If you do not feel peace about keeping the thing, you must get rid of it.

You might not know it is wrong until God convicts you of it. Should He `prick` your heart (like a needle pricking your skin) you will know you must get rid of stuff. I got rid of records, movies, books etc. If you were not raised in a Christian home, please pray over all your sphere of influence. If God brings it to your heart to get rid of something, do it. There is no item that is worth separating you from God. It may have value in the market place but the cost of your soul is too much in comparison to some earthly item.

You know when the Jews prepare for Passover, they can have no leaven in the house. They have to get rid of anything that has leaven in it. They do a thorough search and get rid of it, in remembrance of how Israel was rushed to escape Egypt but command of Pharaoh. It says there
was not even enough time for the dough to rise. God wants there to be no sin in us. His living on the inside of us will cause us to know if there is anything that is not pleasing to Him.

Jesus is coming back to the earth for the Church – His Bride. There cannot be sin in the Church because our bridegroom Jesus is sinless. In fact, He gave His life to purchase His bride.
Ephesians 5: 26 that He might sanctify and cleanse it with the washing of water by the word, 27 and that He might present to Himself a glorious church, not having spot, or wrinkle, or any such thing, but that it should be holy and without blemish.

WARNING

Do not mess with things such as idols or graven images or symbols from a different religion. Don`t have horoscopes as part of your life. These things seem innocent but if you research them, you will see they are all things that go against Jehovah God. Their origin and intent was to go against the most high God. They should not be a part of your life. This in itself could be a separate teaching, but I mention it here because it was a part of my personal testimony and it could be part of yours.

North American Idols

We should have no other gods but Jehovah. You may say, I worship God but I love sports. Sports can be a god to you if you worship it more than God. It doesn`t have to be a god from a different religion. In North America, the big temptation is to worship money. We live in a capitalist society. Our freedoms in democracy also give us privileges to gather wealth. If someone is hard working, he or she can build a company or businesses. The American dream is true in both Canada and the United States. If you do your best, get an education and pursue your dreams, our society gives us freedom to gather wealth. I am thankful for this. I hold it as a cherished part of my society but with it comes the opportunity to abuse it – to put money as more important than God or people. There are people in our society who will steal or kill for money.

Money is not wrong. It is how we do business in our nations. The love of money is the root if all sin (1 Timothy 6: 10). What this means is a lust for money that could cause us to sin – you may say you would never steal or kill for money. Some people sin in different ways such as lie on their income tax or in even smaller ways by cheating someone when the cashier gives you too much change in error. Please see that we must be faithful with matters of money because of the way it could be an idol to us.

Repentance

Repentance means you were going in one direction (away from God) and you realize it is sin. You confess it as sin and receive forgiveness from God. Then you go in a totally new direction.
It literally means a shift in your position so you align with God and God`s direction. You do not return to your former ways. You keep following God. Once God reveals something to you that you know is wrong, you may require ending of old relationships or people who were involved in your life. It is so important who we associate with. Even if they are family members, if they are trying to lead you away from what is right, you must keep them out of your life. This doesn't mean you never see them or care for them but us does mean that you don't let them into your inner circle of trusted close friends. Those closest to you should be people you can share your innermost being with who love God passionately the way you do.

There may be seasons in your life when you are alone. Pray that God would give you opportunities to serve Him more. As you are doing the will of God, the right people will be in your life. They will people you can invest in who can also invest in you. The right people will always manifest as you are seeking God and doing His will.

True Christians are not trying to find ways to live on the edge of what could be acceptable to God and what might not be. Christians who passionately love God repent quickly; they are living their lives with God as the primary focus; all things that are pleasing to God they want. They despise their own sin and pray for mercy, thanking God for the cleansing blood of Calvary – accepting their forgiveness. They know God is Holy and they receive the command to be Holy as He is Holy.

You may wonder if this is possible in our current North American world system. After all the media promotes a very different kind of life one accepting most sins as a normal part of life. If the media is a stumbling block in your life, you must cut it out. This is not a list of what you must do because I said so. This is not keeping rules of a local Church or even trying to be Holy. It is the fruit of Holiness.

If you know that sexual passions arise from watching movies, you must not watch those movies. If you know that your words become negative after listening to different kinds of music, you must avoid that music. You are living in an earthly body that lives by sight, touch, taste, feel, smell, and hearing. Whatever you put into yourself determines what you think about, what you give your affections to, what you accept.

Don't Give in to the Flesh

Pray that God would give you discerning of spirits strong. If you are doing something or partaking of something that grieves the Holy Spirit, ask God to correct you; He will. The Holy spirit will prompt you – you must make the decision to obey. The Holy Spirit is always faithful to do His part; once the Spirit prompts you, you must make an effort to do what is right. It might mean, getting up in the middle of a movie in a theatre and leaving because the movie was profane or obscene. It might mean losing friends who delight in profanity or obscenity. The choice is to do what is best for you. You keeping your own heart is more important than any pleasure or wealth on the earth.

Proverbs 4: 23 Keep your heart with all diligence,
for out of it are the issues of life.
As Adam and Eve were created to care for the Garden of Eden, so must each of us care for the condition of your heart. The innermost part of you was made to commune with God in holiness. You were created to live holy – original sin (the sin all humans are born with) was defeated by the death burial and resurrection of Jesus Christ. Christians do not have to choose to sin. We are making choices constantly; we should be constantly choosing what would draw us closer to Christ.

Important in major decisions but even in the most minor of decisions, don't let any sin separate you from God. Repent quickly. If you get angry and say words you should not have said, repent; if you do something wrong, repent. Ask for Jesus to forgive you. Receive the applied blood of Christ to your life and don't do it again. The only way you or I can live Holy is by constant communion with Christ and living in the Spirit moment by moment.

The First Christian

I know what it is like to be the only Christian in my family. I know what it's like not to have the support of a Christian relationship network. It is tough. Relatives who don't know Christ will not understand you. Friends who don't know Christ will be offering you the opposite of what you need. They are living in the world and following the culture of our world. Don't believe the lie that you are alone. You are not alone.

First, Jesus our High Priest and Intercessor is praying for you. There are millions of born again Spirit filled Christians all over North America and the world. This is where you must get support. Get prayer support from people at your local church. As you become involved in activities at your church, you will meet Christian friends.

Also, there are Christian Ministries that broadcast on the TV, Internet, Satellite etc. I thank God for Christian broadcasting for the blessing it has brought to my life beyond what words can say. The comfort of hearing somebody worshipping God, or preaching or teaching the gospel and Christian news headlines, Christian praise and worship and entertainment has so enriched my life and comforted me, built me up, strengthened me etc. I may never meet these preachers or people face to face on earth but I will be thanking them for what they did on earth in faithfully preaching and teaching etc. because they made all the difference of me feeling included in the Body of Christ.

I have sent prayer requests to many ministries asking for prayer, believing they truly do pray for their partners. The sanctity of this prayer cover, has helped to strengthen me and encourage me. I know angels are released as we pray for each other. I feel a special bond with those ministries that have taught me, encouraged me and built me up.

Iniquity

Repentance is something we should be doing immediately as soon as we know there is any sin. It is also good to pray for your family members, repenting for generational sins. There are often sins that are passed from generation to generation. This comes from lives spent without repenting and developing a hard heart towards sins. The curse of sin is separation from God. Someone living outside of God's protection will become bound by sin and pass these habits, these sins, these iniquities to their children etc. For instance, you may notice many people in your family getting divorced, or in sexual immorality or lying or drunkenness etc.

You as the first Christian can pray and plead the blood of Jesus over your family. You can pray the sins and iniquities end concerning your life and family. You can be a catalyst to your family that they may be saved. Praying for them, that God would soften their hearts and that God would send labourers into their lives sharing Christ with them will put a special wall of protection around them. God can draw them to Himself. You know that if God could save you, He could save anyone.

Repentance for Habitual sins

These sins or iniquities that keep occurring in your life – I mean you repent, you start living right and you sin that same sin again. The Bible refers to this sin as the sin that easily entangles you.
Hebrews 12: 1Therefore, since we are encompassed with such a great cloud of witnesses, let us also lay aside every weight and the sin that so easily entangles us, and let us run with endurance the race that is set before us.

Please know the answer is not beating yourself up about it. Condemnation is of the devil. God doesn't want you condemning yourself. Neither does God want you to be ensnared by those iniquities. The only answer is the blood of Jesus Christ. Keep repenting. Keep pressing into God. Focus on Jesus Christ. Do all you can do to live Holy unto God. Pray for revelation and insight; if necessary, get elders to pray with you for deliverance. The good news is you do not have to stay a slave to any sin. You can be set free. You can live Holy. Jesus Blood – the same blood that saved you – is the same blood that delivers you.

I experienced a radical transformation at salvation. Also, there were things that I fought against. A tremendous truth was imparted to me through Marilyn Hickey teaching on deliverance. She said to pray out loud over yourself, " God if I do that sin…NAME IT… let me thrown up and become violently ill. That is how much I want to be free from it." Once you're ready to pray that type of prayer, you can expect results that will transform you. The chains fall off as you magnify Jesus.

Don't focus on not doing the sin. Some churches focus on not doing the sins repeatedly. In fact they become so sin conscious that they are in the realm of legalism. By focusing on the wrong thing, they become a filthy work of the flesh. You would actually think you deserved salvation because you kept those commandments. Focus on Jesus the Saviour, The LORD, the only Omnipotent God. This brings freedom. Jesus came to set the captives free.

Luke 4: "The Spirit of the Lord is upon Me,
because He has anointed Me
to preach the gospel to the poor;
He has sent Me to heal the broken-hearted,
to preach deliverance to the captives
and recovery of sight to the blind,
to set at liberty those who are oppressed;
19 to preach the acceptable year of the Lord."[e]

Jesus not only forgives you for sin, but He also, breaks the power of sins' ability to attract you. The more you focus on Jesus Christ and press in with all your spirit to know Him, the freer you will live. Once you receive forgiveness for sin and deliverance also, don't keep focusing on it – instead fix your eyes upon Jesus. As you live your life for Jesus and live in a Christian Church with the fellowship of Christian family or friends, you will be living unto the LORD. There will be less sinning. It isn't the goal – the goal is to follow Jesus and cast off anything that would be a hindrance to you.

Be Merciful

Never believe that you earned your way. Only the blood of Christ and mercy of God could set you free. You can only boast in the goodness of God towards you. Be merciful to Christians who sin and lose their way. Pray that God would give you compassion for those who are backslidden. They once knew the glory of God, but now they are living in sin. They can never be happy in sin if they have ever known God.

Restore Such a one

Galatians 6: 1 Brothers, if a man is caught in any transgression, you who are spiritual should restore such a one in the spirit of meekness, watching yourselves, lest you also be tempted. 2 Bear one another's burdens, and so fulfill the law of Christ.

It is essential that mature Christians keep humble. We should also pray and care for the sheep that have gone astray. Not only the pastor but the people should care if someone who once knew God is living in sin. You cannot restore anybody but Jesus Christ living in you and through you can.

There have been several of these occasions for myself. I knew that I knew it was God using me and in situation I was humbled to the point of tears upon speaking with the individuals. God's compassion for those people filled my heart and I knew the love of Christ for them more than any sin they could have ever committed. I saw them with unconditional love – not my own – with compassion in light of their eternal soul. I reached out to those people at God's prompting, but I completely say it was not my own words, or love or sharing that was effective.

Only the Spirit of God filling me and using me enabled me to speak words that caused those individuals to repent and return to God. I knew that I knew it was God and not me. I knew that I knew that my own human love was short of the passionate desire to restore them to the body of Christ that welled up in my being. Only God can restore anyone. Never think it was you. Always give God the glory. Offer yourself as a humble offering to reach out with mercy. Consider your own soul – remembering what Christ has saved you from. Reach to restore as scripture instructs.

If you know that a brother or sister was wounded or offended by someone and has stopped going to church, you should do something. Praying is right, but you might also need to go speak to the person. Often the simplest words are the hardest to say. Submit yourself to God as a vessel He can use and ask God to use you in bringing peace and restoration to that person. Willingness to be used, humility and maturity are necessary.

Reach towards the person. Ask God to use you. Be direct with whatever Jesus has you to say or do. If God has placed that person on your heart, He will soften that person's heart. If the person doesn't listen to you, obey Matt 18: 15-19. If the person rejects you, is offended or sinful and won't repent. Bring an elder with you next. Pray that God will restore that person. If the person still rejects you and the elder, get the Pastor. If the person becomes so hard hearted that he or she will not repent, leave the person.

Persisting Faith

I say leave the person, but it doesn't mean you have to stop praying for the person. It doesn't mean you never reach towards them again. I know of people who out right sinned and left the Church but there were friends and pastors who refused to give up on them. They persisted and persisted and persisted and eventually the back-sliders confessed their sins and returned to the LORD. You must be led by the Holy Spirit in all things, and in restoring a person to God, it is essential. The Holy Spirit using you – God using you is the only way you could be effective. Name calling, arguing, anger – any fleshly emotion can never produce a fruit of righteousness. Since we are born from the spirit of God and have His spirit in us – we must be led by the Spirit.

Prayer

The reason I am imparting this message is because God can soften someone's heart. Pray for the person for one more chance to repent; that God will send a Christian to him or her that will share Christ. Pray that God will put Christians next to them in the workplace or in their neighborhoods. Pray they may watch TV preaching and give their lives to Christ. As you and I pray for people, God releases angels to perform the word. God will never violate a human will by forcing people to accept Him but He will give them more opportunities to receive Christ, as we pray and intercede for them. They may not listen to you, but God knows how to reach people. He found a way to reach you; He can save any one.

The moment a person repents is not when Jesus forgave the person. Jesus forgave the person when he died on the cross and rose from the dead. Jesus forgiveness must be accepted now though. The person must say "Thank you God you died for my sin so I could be free." The person must receive the blood of Jesus as the only answer to sin. The person once repentant is transformed, changed, quickened, strengthened.

## 11 PRAYING IN TONGUES

The good news is that if you have not been baptized in the Holy Spirit speaking in other tongues – you can be. You must believe that Jesus is your Saviour – you must pray in faith believing that the gift of the baptism of the Holy Spirit with the evidence of speaking in tongues is for today. What happens is that you press in as close as you can get to God wanting more of Him and He fills you to overflowing with His Spirit. You may shake or tremble; you may be slain in the spirit (fall down); you may start crying or laughing; you may simply continue praising God from English and you hear the words to speak in a different language and start doing it.

As you were baptized or immersed in water for water baptism, so are you immersed in the Holy Spirit in the Baptism of the Holy Spirit. You will begin to speak in languages you have never learned. There are two types of this expression: one is praying in an unknown language only known by God. Sometimes God will reveal to you what you are saying. The origin is the Holy Spirit. This gift is used in the church sometimes.

The second expression is similar, you are speaking in a language you haven't learned but it is a language of the earth, of a different people. This was the use on the day of Pentecost as the 120 were gathered in the upper room were filled with the Spirit, immersed in the Spirit so strongly that they were compelled to go into the streets praising and worshipping God in these new languages. (Acts 2) The pilgrims were gathered to celebrate Pentecost and they heard the 120 praising God in their own languages from different regions and nations.

You can be baptized in the Holy Spirit by praying for it. It is a gift of God and so you should desire it. You may ask God for it and He can fill you to overflowing. You may receive it by pressing into God and wanting more of Him. You may not even know what has happened to you. That is what happened to me as a new Christian.

My own testimony

I had been saved for approximately 2 or 3 months. I had no Bible teaching – only preaching from the pulpit. I was not from a Christian home. Every service I attended, I felt drawn to go pray at the altar. I prayed and praised God that day. The Minister speaking was visiting and was asking people to commit their lives to live for Christ all their lives.

He let us know it was serious and might mean going to be a missionary or to do anything God prompted us to do. I felt the tugging of God at my heart so strong, I nearly ran to the altar area. There were thousands of people there – you couldn't get close to the platform. I committed myself wholly to follow the LORD asking for all of Him, praying to know Him more, desiring more of Him. I was worshipping God and surrendering my life to Him as I started speaking in a different language I didn't know. It wasn't scary – it was unique. My friend was standing near to me and it scared her so she left me there. I was oblivious to all other surroundings – I was fixed on seeking God and worshipping Him.

I mentioned what happened to the friend who lead me to Christ and she explained to me what it was. Please know I was a new Christian, not yet baptized in water but wholly desiring God; God mercifully baptized me in the Holy Spirit.

The Presence of God

Most people who experience this will say they have felt the presence of the LORD very strong; they were filled with peace; they were worshipping to overflowing. This means you worship and you worship and you worship and all you want to do is stay in the presence of God. It is hard to find natural words to describe what spiritually occurs. Literally, it is God Himself filling us with Himself so that we are flowing in the Holy Spirit with our spirit. I would describe it as a fountain that is flowing with the well-spring of water deeply within you; there is no ending to the glory that keeps bubbling up. Jesus said (John 4) that He would give us water that would never stop flowing.

Let's look here in Acts 2: 1- 4. It describes the way the disciples were baptized in the Holy Spirit.

Acts 2: 1 When the day of Pentecost had come, they were all together in one place. 2 Suddenly a sound like a mighty rushing wind came from heaven, and it filled the whole house where they were sitting. 3 There appeared to them tongues as of fire, being distributed and resting on each of them, 4 and they were all filled with the Holy Spirit and began to speak in other tongues, as the Spirit enabled them to speak.

The Disciples Who Received the Baptism of the Holy Spirit

These disciples had witnessed Jesus Resurrected from the dead. Many of them saw Him visibly ascend into heaven surrounded by angels. Jesus instructed them to wait in Jerusalem for the gift of the Holy Spirit. They obeyed and gathered in the upper room praying for what Jesus promised; the Spirit of God was poured on them. This occasion was unique and I know of no other occasion in scripture or in testimony where little tongues of fire – or lamps of fire were evident above people's heads. It occurred that day so they could see it. It was the fulfillment of the promise of the gift of the Spirit (Joel 2) that would empower them to preach and teach Christ so that all people could know that Jesus is the Saviour of all people.

I have heard of instances with the outpouring of the spirit where people saw a supernatural glow or light or radiance – but not exactly the same as on the day of Pentecost. It was a sign to the believing Jews who gathered at Pentecost; it was a sign to the disciple themselves that God had fulfilled His promise and it was a sign to us who read God's Word that we might know our God is mighty and desires to pour His Spirit upon us even though we are living in temporal bodies. I would compare this event in importance to God appearing to Moses in the burning bush. It radically changed the nations.

Your first speaking in tongues may be compared to a baby who is learning his or her natural language. There may be syllables; there may be phrases; there might not be a full flow. Some people, its like a gusher, a fountain springing in full use; others, it starts slowly as you yield to the Holy Spirit. The more you pray in tongues, the smoother the flow will be. You may have recurring phrases that God gives to you especially. It is like a natural language because there are words, phrases etc.

The Groanings of the Spirit

The gift of tongues is not simply for feeling the presence of God. Please let me add, if that were the only benefit, I would desire it so strongly anyway. But there is an impartation of God's Spirit filling our human spirit so that we are praying the perfect will of God.

Romans 8: 26 Likewise, the Spirit helps us in our weaknesses, for we do not know what to pray for as we ought, but the Spirit Himself intercedes for us with groanings too deep for words. 27 He who searches the hearts knows what the mind of the Spirit is, because He intercedes for the saints according to the will of God.

Please understand this. I am saying that the Holy Spirit living inside us – fills us to overflowing so that we start praying the perfect will of God for ourselves or others. The groanings of the Spirit lead us to pray – we may not always know what we are praying for; sometimes though God reveals to us an interpretation of the tongue or words of knowledge about the tongue we are speaking.

On the day of Pentecost, the 120 were praising God and went out into the streets of Jerusalem praising God in their new tongues. Over 2, 000 people got saved. People from other nations, heard God being praised in their own language by men who were fishermen not scholars. Peter preaches a sermon about Jesus as Messiah and his death, burial and resurrection. The people respond with faith and the church is multiplied exponentially because of the Baptism of the Holy Spirit.

A Sign to Those who Want to Know God

The Baptism of the Holy Spirit empowers us to preach or teach Christ. The gifts of the Spirit help us to build up the body of Christ. The fruit of the Spirit makes our lives living examples of God's character in the earth. The early church multiplied at a rapid rate.

As it was in the book of Acts, so it is today. The manifest out pouring of the Holy Spirit in the church causes people to want to be there. Most people will know it is wondrous and desire to know more. We should not be trying to spare the visitors from the gifts of the Spirit. The gifts of the Spirit will attract people and cause them to want to know God. They are given to us so that we could minister. The church will multiply if the gifts of the Spirit are in the church. The Lord will add to the church as we pursue Him.

1 Corinthians 12: 4 There are various gifts, but the same Spirit. 5 There are differences of administrations, but the same Lord. 6 There are various operations, but it is the same God who operates all of them in all people.7 But the manifestation of the Spirit is given to everyone for the common good. 8 To one is given by the Spirit the word of wisdom, to another the word of knowledge by the same Spirit, 9 to another faith by the same Spirit, to another gifts of healings by the same Spirit, 10 to another the working of miracles, to another prophecy, to another discerning of spirits, to another various kinds of tongues, and to another the interpretation of tongues. 11 But that one and very same Spirit works all these, dividing to each one individually as He will.

Somebody baptized in the Holy Spirit, who is praying in the Spirit (praying in tongues earnestly) is someone God can use in divergent ways. You may be praying about something that will occur in your day and give you grace or cause you to assist someone in need. God can give you words or phrases in the interpretation of tongues that you may share with someone or that will encourage you. And you praise and pray in tongues, the other gifts of the Holy Spirit are released with fresh strength. You will feel compelled to give or serve, or teach or encourage or prophesy. The gifts are evidence of the Spirit living on the inside of you.

Each Christian has gifts and talents that God has given them; the Baptism of the Holy Spirit releases these people to minister in the body of Christ and also in the world they live in. God can use you to impact your community; your school; your workplace; your home; your family; all spheres of society – wherever you go, God can use you to be a witness of His glory, His mercy and His compassion.

Life in the Spirit

The Holy Spirit is the medium that God uses to do spiritual activity on earth. For instance, I am typing this message; I could speak or preach this message; I could do a live session in front of people or I could tape it and record a DVD. Those are all mediums for the message on prayer that I am sharing, In this instance, my book, is the medium I am using. In the same way, God uses the Holy Spirit to do spiritual things on the earth through us. If there is a demand on the gift, and we are living in the spirit, the Spirit will manifest the gift and the person will receive the answer to his or her faith. It usually results in miracles, healings, lives transformed.

I Would that you All Prophesy

1 Corinthians 14: 5 I desire that you all speak in tongues, but even more that you prophesy. For greater is he who prophesies than he who speaks in tongues, unless he interprets, so that the church may receive edification.

The Apostle Paul is the author who gives us church order. We who are Christians get our order of service from the Apostle Paul and the early Church. Paul is saying he wishes they all spoke in other tongues. There must be a reason for it. Usually, this verse is used only to emphasize – that even more so you would prophesy but I am saying if it wasn't important Paul wouldn't say he wanted them all to do it. The gift is for all people not only some. Whoever wants the gift and asks God for it, will receive it.

18 I thank my God that I speak in tongues more than you all. 19 Yet in the church I had rather speak five words with my understanding, that by my voice I might teach others also, than ten thousand words in an unknown tongue.

There are places God uses us in our gifts: in our homes (in private) and in public in the church or in the marketplace your spheres of influence on the earth. God often deals with us in private as we are praising or praying in tongues and gives us revelation or insight into our day.

Although your first utterances in tongues may be simple syllables or words or phrases likened to a baby uttering his or her first words, we are not made to stay in an infant stage of tongues. As we use the gift of tongues to worship or praise or pray, our prayer language will develop as a steady flow. We will utter what the Spirit brings to us and we will get boldness knowing it is God speaking through us or praying through us. We will not get the full benefit of tongues if we do not use the gift often. It is meant for us to use regularly, so much that the Apostle Paul says I thank God that I pray in tongues more than you all. (1 Corinthians 14: 18) He is letting us know this gift is very important.

The Gift of Tongues in the Church Service

It is true Paul says the gift of prophecy should be desired so that we might build up the church, but that does not take away from the importance of using the gift of tongues. Sometimes in a service someone will profoundly feel to give an utterance in tongues. What will usually happen is that person or another person will pray for the interpretation and speak it to the church afterwards. A different person might get the revelation of the interpretation and speak it out. If it is not right away, the pastor will often ask the congregation to pray for an interpretation. That is the proper use of the gift of tongues used in a church service.

By yourself though, you can be praying in tongues and knowing God is using you. If you feel a desire to know what you are praying, as you are praying in tongues also ask God to give you understanding of the matter. He will give it to you. It is not for anyone but yourself to know how the spirit is praying through you.

Place for Praying in Tongues in the Church

Standing at you seat or at the alter praying, as you yield to the Holy Spirit praying and praising in tongues, it quickens the other gifts of the Spirit. The gift of faith, gift of working of miracles, gift or prophecy etc. begin to be released and we may start ministering to those around us or feel a strong desire to do so. This is how the body of Christ was created – so that each part build up the other parts. As you are flowing the in Holy Spirit, you will desire to impart something to those around you. If we did this in our churches – pray in the Spirit as a Church, pray in the Spirit at the altar, the gifts of the spirit would be manifest in our churches.

Oh it is good to praise the LORD and pray with understanding in the language that you speak, but there is a place of congregational prayer in tongues and ministry to people at the altar with tongues. This directly connects you to the giftings of God. If you are praying for somebody but you don't know what to say, start praying in tongues; God will move upon you with wisdom, words of wisdom, words of knowledge and discerning of spirits.

Special Holy Spirit Lead Worship in Tongues

Sometimes with an anointed prophetic worship leader, a song of the LORD may rise, praising God in tongues and with understanding. I've been in strong meetings where all the church will start worshipping in tongues and a new song in understanding will come forth and all the congregation will be singing the song the LORD has given the worship leader. This type of Holy Spirit lead atmosphere will be conductive to all sorts of gifts being activated and some people being instantly healed or set free. The gift of tongues and praising and worship in tongues is not for no reason – it releases faith, the manifest presence of God and the giftings within believers.

Apostolic Anointing

A special faith is released during these spiritual meetings and if an Apostle of God is leading, special faith and special miracles will be released in the service. Often the Apostle will be able to discern what should occur whether it is a special word of knowledge for the congregation or scriptures or a call for healing or a Jericho march around the church. The Apostle's direction will help to manifest God's will for that service and that congregation.

I would compare it to this. I have been in the Toronto train station on many occasions. I know it well. Should I see a picture of it or should I be there, I know my way around because I have been there so often. If suddenly I were transported into the midst of the Toronto train station, I would know exactly where I was – even though it would be weird – I would notice the familiar because I know the place.

The Apostle is much like this in the realms of the spirit because the Apostle is someone who presses into the Spirit and lives in the realms of God's glory. He or she, can spiritually discern the moving of the Holy Spirit and perceive what God wants to do in the service. How does he or she know?

Because the Apostle lives in the realm of the spirit and is given authority to use in the congregation to lead and guide the congregation and to release the giftings in the Prophet, Pastor, Teacher and Evangelist. The gifts of the spirit are released as faith is released in believers' hearts.

During these types of meetings, people will repent without anyone asking them to. People will start crying; people will be healed physically. People may receive forgiveness. People may decide to become missionaries. People may be set free from smoking or drinking or drugs. People will feel the presence of God and want to get right with God. Spirit manifest spirit. As you are praising and worshipping or praying in tongues, God can manifest in whatever you have need of.

Ephesians 6: 18 Pray in the Spirit always with all kinds of prayer and supplication.

Stir up your own self in the spirit.

In your home, as you pray, make part of your prayer a stirring of the gifts of the Spirit. We are instructed to stir up spiritual gifts. (2 Timothy 1: 6) You do this by literally praying over yourself and saying " I stir up the gift of faith. Gift of faith spring up – come forth." You do that over yourself regularly with all the gifts, God will be using you at church or at home or in the marketplace. Roberts Liardon, a mighty preacher and church historian has an excellent teaching on this topic of stirring up your gifts. If you could get a chance to listen to it, I highly recommend it to you. You can pray over yourself in your natural language and you can pray over yourself in tongues.

The Gift of Tongues

God gives us the gifts but we must stir them up; we must use them. It is possible to be baptized in the Holy Spirit and not to use the gift. It is possible to have the gifts of God but not stir them. It is possible that you may ignore them or not use them. The Holy Spirit will never force you to speak in tongues or force you to use any spiritual gift. The Holy Spirit is our teacher, our helper; He will prompt us but God highly regards our human will and will never violate it. Praying in tongues and the baptism of the Holy Spirit is the miraculous realm. It is an empowering for the service of Christ. If you ever don't know how to pray for yourself or someone, literally start praying in tongues, believing God will show you what to pray.

Years ago, I heard Kenneth Hagin Senior preach and give a challenge. He challenged anyone who needed a miracle form God to pray in tongues 1 hour a day for 30 days. He said that if someone did this but didn't get answer to pray to write him. I took his challenge praying in tongues, more and more each day. I never wrote him. I knew a key to life in the Spirit had been revealed to me and that God was speaking to me more and using me more because I was pressing in to Him with all my being and praying in tongues every day.

Because I was praying in tongues, I began dreaming dreams, seeing visions, being directed to pray for people; God would use me more; I would go for a walk someone would be there – I would share Christ frequently with strangers. My life was given to prayer, praise and evangelism. I also would get supernatural words of wisdom and knowledge concerning my own self and those around me.

The Baptism of the Holy Spirit with speaking in other tongues is for ourselves, but it is also to build up the Church. It is to help prepare the Body of Christ for Christ's return. God wants to use you; give yourself to God wholly: spirit soul and body; expect God to use you. Praying in tongues requires you living in the Spirit and being led by the Spirit.

Chris Legebow

## COMMENTS

This study in kinds of prayer is to help you know which prayers to pray in various situations. You would not have read this book if you didn't want to pray for yourself and for others. Please use this book as a refresher to your faith as you live your life as a Christian intercessor.

Keep connected to other people who pray. Keep consistently praying about the people, animals. Situations God impresses on your heart. You are given the choice to make a difference for God's glory by your willingness to pray. Be encouraged. Thank God when you receive an answer to prayer. Celebrate the victories with others of like precious faith. Invite the Holy Spirit to lead you and guide you in various types of prayer. The Holy spirit will prompt you and direct you. Let the Holy Spirit be your senior partner.

## CLOSING PRAYER:

O Holy Spirit quicken the things in this book that are inspired by you to the reader that it would come to his or her remembrance. Let him or her be enlightened to know the kinds of prayer most effective for their situations.

Give them wisdom and strong discerning of spirits. O God anoint the readers to desire you more and to press into you more that they may intercede for people, for animals, for nations and situations small or big. Nothing is too small that you don't care about it. Nothing is too big that you can't intervene and bring the solution to it.

God pour out a Spirit of intercession, supplication and intercession on those who have read this book. Draw your people to prayer that we may have revival in our nations.

You said if your people would humble themselves and pray, you would hear from heaven and answer and bring healing to our nation. (2 Chronicles 7: 14)

I pray protection over the readers. I plead the blood over them that as they press in to know you more, you will protect them and use them for your glory as members of Your Church. Amen.

# Chris Legebow

# ABOUT THE AUTHOR

Chris Legebow is a Christian Professor of English and Communications. She has taught at the elementary, high school and College and University levels. She has ministered in her local churches in intercessory prayer, teaching Sunday school and other Christian Doctrine classes to children and youths. She has preached to congregations and given her testimony. Although she was not raised in a Christian home, she came to know Jesus Christ as her Saviour and LORD while she was studying in University. This radically transformed her life in terms of priorities and commitment.

She has a strong passion for the great commission – that Jesus Christ would be preached throughout all the earth believing that it a major sign of the LORD's return. She has been a part of several different types of full gospel charismatic churches but has also gained much of her insight and enlightenment from Christian Media and broadcasting. She hopes to continue ministering, serving, interceding and giving and teaching until the LORD returns.

www.ingramcontent.com/pod-product-compliance
Lightning Source LLC
Chambersburg PA
CBHW031551040426
42452CB00006B/267